The ADVENTURE

ALSO BY STEVE TAYLOR

The Fall

Making Time

Waking from Sleep

Out of the Darkness

Back to Sanity

The Meaning

Not I, Not Other Than I (as editor)

The Calm Center

The Leap

Spiritual Science

The Clear Light

Extraordinary Awakenings

DisConnected

• An Eckhart Tolle Edition •

The ADVENTURE

A Practical Guide to Spiritual Awakening

STEVE TAYLOR

Foreword by ECKHART TOLLE

New World Library
Novato, California

FOREWORD

The only viable path ahead for humanity is that of awakening — or wakefulness, as Steve Taylor puts it. Fortunately, with each passing year, ever more people are finding access to that state: pure, unconditioned consciousness and the expansive peace and heightened sense of aliveness that it gives rise to. Taylor is one of a growing number of teachers who have devoted their lives to promoting that state in as many people as possible, and this book, *The Adventure*, is his latest contribution to that endeavor. In it, he makes the crucial point that wakefulness is not reserved for gurus or ascetics cloistered in monasteries but is, in fact, quite common and within reach of every person.

All his previous works have in their own way provided invaluable signposts pointing the way toward the path of awakening — be it through his poetic reflections that serve as windows into presence or through his presentations of research into the multitudinous experiences of those who have attained and maintain wakefulness. *The Adventure* is different and perhaps even more potent in that it provides specific, accessible guidelines and practices that enable readers to embark and progress on the path for themselves. More than mere signposts, it offers a loose itinerary to follow, even a vehicle for the journey, for all those who wish to live out their unique version of this greatest adventure, the awakening of consciousness.

At the outset, Taylor delineates the eight qualities of wakefulness and offers guidelines for the journey. He then devotes one chapter to each of the qualities. Together, they provide "a raft to take us across," a means of getting from the normal human state of denial or forgetfulness of the Now — that is to say, misery — to the presence, peace, and joy of being.

Taylor writes, "all qualities of wakefulness naturally grow stronger as we practice them." And so the chapters include meditations and poems to encourage the integration of the qualities, as well as occasional stories from Taylor's own life and those of awakened people he has interviewed. They also present two types of practical exercises: contemplative exercises and life practices.

While solitary contemplation is essential, life practices are arguably more so, because, as Taylor puts it, "everyday life provides many excellent opportunities for spiritual growth that a monastery cannot"; indeed, one of his foundational guidelines is "everyday life is part of the adventure." It must be, for otherwise you will not be in charge of your own journey but rather like a passenger on a bus speeding along a narrow cliffside road, at the mercy of an intoxicated driver with one hand on the wheel and the other typing messages on his smartphone. Clearly, that's the wrong kind of adventure! Instead, by doing these practices, you will build the skill of catching yourself when you react to life's unpredictable events and inevitable challenges by slipping out of awareness and into drama, boredom, self-recrimination, or any other manifestation of the mind's tendency to veer into past or future.

If you follow this book's guidance, your life's journey can become what it is meant to be: "a glorious adventure, full of grace and joy," one in which you are present in the Now and therefore stop to smell the roses, ever aware of the beauty and the miracle of life continuously unfolding all around you. In this way, you can transcend ego, thought chatter, the pain-body — our inherited dysfunction — and contribute to the flowering of human consciousness, the evolutionary leap that is the only way humanity can overcome the seemingly insurmountable problems we face.

— Eckhart Tolle, bestselling author of
The Power of Now and *A New Earth*

INTRODUCTION

The Adventure is a book of spiritual guidance, containing exercises, discussions, and meditations, all designed to cultivate spiritual awakening. It assumes that wakefulness — or enlightenment, if you prefer — is accessible to us all and will inevitably arise if we follow certain practices and develop certain qualities.

This book grew out of a series of workshops and online courses linked to my earlier book *The Leap: The Psychology of Spiritual Awakening. The Leap* was primarily descriptive, based on my studies of people who underwent a gradual or sudden shift into wakefulness. The book also drew on my own spiritual experiences and my studies of the world's spiritual traditions. I examined the different ways in which awakening can occur and the various characteristics of the wakeful state.

To use a metaphor, the primary purpose of *The Leap* was to describe the landscape of wakefulness, whereas the primary purpose of this book is to show you how to *reach* the landscape. At my workshops and courses, I didn't just want to talk about spiritual awakening; I wanted to enable my participants to *experience* it. I wanted the participants to touch into the heightened awareness, harmony, connectedness, and sense of gratitude that arise in wakefulness. I wanted to show them that these qualities can be cultivated in their everyday lives. To this end, I offered them exercises and meditations to take away and use on a daily basis. These exercises and meditations form the basis of this book.

Here — as in my workshops — I focus on eight qualities or characteristics of wakefulness. The essential principle is that to cultivate these individual characteristics means to cultivate wakefulness itself, as an overall state. You could compare it to the state of health, which depends on a number of different factors, such as exercise, diet, sleep, a positive mental outlook, and so on. If you want to cultivate an overall state of health, you have to work on each of these factors. If you exercise, have a good diet, sleep well, and are relatively free of mental stress, then you're more likely to attain an overall state of health. It's not enough to focus on just one or two aspects — you have to work on them all. The same applies to wakefulness.

I devote a chapter to each of the eight qualities of wakefulness: disidentification from the ego, gratitude, presence, altruism, acceptance, integration with the body, dissolving psychological attachments, and embracing our mortality. Each chapter includes guidance, exercises, and meditations to help you cultivate the characteristics. (I will provide some instructions on how to use the exercises in chapter 1.)

These eight qualities certainly aren't the only characteristics of wakefulness. In *The Leap*, I highlighted several others, such as heightened awareness, transcendence of separation, inner quietness, and authentic relationships. I have chosen to focus on the eight qualities named above for two reasons. First, they are simple and overt characteristics that, as my workshops have shown, can be directly cultivated through exercises and practices. Other prominent characteristics are more abstruse and difficult to directly cultivate.

Second, and more importantly, the eight qualities are core or source characteristics of wakefulness that incorporate and engender other qualities. In other words, once we establish these qualities as a foundation, then the other characteristics — including heightened awareness and a transcendence of separation — will naturally emerge too. As we go along, I will discuss some of these emergent qualities, and I will also summarize them in the final chapter of the book.

It's also important to understand the wider context of awakening: what it means, how and why it occurs, and where it leads. I therefore frame the eight main chapters with introductory and concluding chapters that discuss this wider context.

THE PRACTICAL ASPECT

Many spiritual teachers and authors describe the process of awakening (and enlightenment itself) with great insight, also identifying some of the obstacles that prevent us from awakening. However, some teachers don't offer much guidance on how to actually *attain* wakefulness. Spiritual teachings often overlook the practical aspect.

It's all well and good to state that we are all one, that we are all manifestations of awareness or spirit, and that all we need to do is to become aware of our oneness or our essential spiritual nature. But if we don't know how to attain that state, these teachings are not particularly helpful. We might feel blissful in the presence of a teacher; we might gain clarity and wisdom while reading their books. But what happens when we're back in our everyday lives, in the office or factory or dealing with our young kids or elderly parents? How do we integrate the teachings into our daily lives? To adapt a metaphor used by the Buddha, it's not enough to describe the other side of the river or to point at it — we need a raft to take us across.

Some teachers even claim that there is nothing we can *do* to wake up. They reason that the notion of awakening implies an achievement, a future goal to strive toward, which strengthens the very ego that we're supposed to transcend. In essence, such teachers state, we are already awakened, and it is our striving that stops our essential wakefulness from manifesting itself. In terms of the Buddha's metaphor, we're on the other side of the river already and so don't need a raft. All we really need to do is to let go of the spiritual search and realize where we already are.

This sounds beautiful, but it rarely, if ever, works. More often than not, if we don't follow any practices or strategies of awakening, our constricting psychological patterns remain intact, maintaining our normal sleep state and prolonging our suffering and discord. In an absolute sense, it's true that we are already awakened. But most human beings are alienated from our spiritual essence. It takes much more than abandoning the spiritual search to gain access to our essence and cultivate ongoing wakefulness.

So in this book, I go to great lengths to be practical. As a psychologist, I know that specific psychological changes need to occur if we are to transcend our normal sleep state. Through my research, I know that there are certain qualities we can develop in order to move toward wakefulness. I offer guidance and practices that I know are effective, because I have seen their fruits during my workshops and courses.

Awakening is the greatest adventure we can undertake as human beings. It's a voyage of discovery that reveals exhilarating beauty and richness but may also expose us to challenges. It's amazing that human beings have climbed to the top of Mount Everest. It's even more amazing that we've traveled to the moon. But greater still is the adventure of self-transformation, of expanding our awareness, opening ourselves to a greater reality, transcending separation, and becoming more connected to ourselves, to other living beings, to nature and the whole cosmos.

At this time in history, when the external world has been almost exhaustively explored and conquered, it's surely the right time for us to reverse our attention and undertake the inward journey of self-exploration and self-transformation. Indeed, in the light of the present crises faced by our species, our very survival may depend on our collective awakening.

I'm looking forward to being your guide on this great adventure.

1

GUIDELINES

Beginning the Adventure

Before you begin a journey, it's useful to have an idea of where you're going. It's helpful to have some directions, some knowledge of the types of terrain you'll encounter, and some notion of the changes and challenges you may meet along the way. This is especially important for the spiritual journey, as the landscape of wakefulness is unfamiliar to many of us.

Of course, many other spiritual explorers have made the journey before us and have left maps. Numerous spiritual traditions, such as Buddhism, Sufism, Taoism, and Christian mysticism, offer helpful guidelines and descriptions. Some of these descriptions might seem rather obscure and even seem to differ slightly from each other, as they are clothed in the concepts and beliefs of their specific traditions. Nevertheless, they all point in the same general direction: beyond separation, toward oneness; beyond discord, toward harmony; beyond suffering, toward peace.

My approach isn't linked to any particular tradition. I respect all spiritual traditions and feel a great affinity with many of them (especially Buddhism and Hindu Vedanta). However, I feel that the best approach is to view awakening outside the context of traditions. You could compare spiritual traditions to walkers in different locations in the same landscape. As each observes the landscape from their specific vantage point, they describe it in slightly different ways. Nevertheless, it's always the same landscape. All their perspectives are equally valid.

However, I try to describe the landscape of wakefulness in a more neutral and naked state, unfiltered by different beliefs and cultures. I also try to describe the landscape in overview, beyond any particular perspective. I convey the essential principles and practices shared by most of the traditions.

My nontraditional approach stems partly from my research. As well as following my own journey of awakening throughout my life, I have spent many years studying cases of spiritual awakening as a psychologist. My research has shown that wakefulness is much more common than most people realize. It is not a rare and esoteric state that has only ever been attained by a small number of monks, mystics, and gurus. It happens to ordinary people in the midst of everyday life, often to people who don't know anything about spirituality and have never followed any spiritual practices.

Spontaneous awakening is usually connected to intense psychological turmoil, such as bereavement, depression, addiction, or the distress caused by serious illness. (My book *Extraordinary Awakenings* is about this type of awakening.) In such cases, a person's normal identity collapses under the pressure of the turmoil or slowly dismantles over a long period of loss and trauma. For most people, this simply equates to a breakdown, but for some, it allows a latent spiritually awakened self to emerge, like a phoenix from the ashes of the ego. This new self becomes established as their new normal identity.

In this book, I will take you on a more gradual, gentle journey. We will slowly transform ourselves through a process of identifying patterns and processes, removing obstacles, changing perspectives, softening boundaries, expanding awareness, and transcending limitations.

I'll now offer you several guidelines to prepare for the adventure of awakening.

GUIDELINE 1: AWAKENING IS AN EXPANSION OF AWARENESS

First, let's consider what it means to awaken, so that we can understand the journey that we're undertaking.

Awakening means an expansion and intensification of awareness across different areas. We experience an intensification of perception, which means that the world around us becomes more real and beautiful. It's as if a veil falls away and a rich, new layer of reality reveals itself, shining with radiance and freshness.

Awakening also means expanding *inner* awareness. We transcend ego separateness and become aware of deeper aspects of our being, including potentials and energies we never sensed before. Imagine a person who lives in a tiny room in the middle of a large house. He has always assumed that the room is the whole of his living space and has never ventured outside it. But now he realizes that many other floors and rooms exist beneath, above, and around him, all of which he is free to explore.

In addition, awakening means expanding and intensifying our relationship to others. Our awareness is no longer confined to our own minds and bodies. It spreads out, allowing us to enter the consciousness of others and of the world itself. This means that we feel more empathy and compassion for others. We can sense their feelings, their pain and joy, and so become careful to avoid hurting them. On the contrary, we feel a strong impulse to help others, to alleviate their suffering and encourage their development.

Finally, awakening means an expansion of perspective. It means developing a wide-ranging, global view of the world in place of an egocentric outlook. Our circle of concern grows, embracing the well-being of others, of whole societies, and of the entire world. Social and global issues become at least as important as our own personal problems. We also gain a clear sense of what is essential and what isn't. We're no longer preoccupied with trivial matters like possessions, success, keeping up appearances, or competing with others. We become more focused on really important issues, such as helping others, contributing to the world, using our creativity, or exploring our spirituality. As one awakened person told me, "Trivial things seem more trivial, and important things seem more important." (The contemplative exercises in this book are mostly designed to expand our perspective in this sense.)

One can also view awakening as a process of opening. In our normal state — what I call our sleep state — we are closed off: closed off to the reality of the world around us, closed off to the fullness of our own being, and closed off to the consciousness of others. We exist in separateness, with strong boundaries between us and the rest of the world. But in awakening, we open up and connect more profoundly to the world around us, to our deep inner being, and to people and other living beings.

As our awareness expands and intensifies, we attain a higher-functioning, more harmonious state. We transcend the discord and suffering that plague human beings in the normal sleep state. We feel a fundamental sense of wholeness and well-being, which means that life becomes much easier and more fulfilling.

This is the process of expansion and opening that you will undergo as we move through the chapters of this book.

GUIDELINE 2: SPIRITUAL AWAKENING IS NOT A GOAL

The impulse to awaken is not egoic. It doesn't mean striving to reach a goal in the same way that we might strive to be successful or wealthy. This impulse is much bigger than the ego. It stems from the deepest levels of our being, beyond our personal desires and goals. It's an evolutionary impulse to expand awareness, together with a natural impulse to grow from discord toward harmony or from suffering toward peace. To follow this impulse is to align ourselves with life itself.

However, the journey of awakening can sometimes be hijacked by the ego. I once met a young spiritual seeker who told me that he was determined to become enlightened by the age of thirty. To this end, he made a list of spiritual texts to read and planned to meditate for a minimum of five hours a day. That young man must be well past thirty now, but I very much doubt that he has attained enlightenment (unless he has changed his approach!). Seeking enlightenment is not like wanting to become a millionaire or a famous pop star. The more you consciously desire it, the less likely you are to attain it.

The important thing is simply to flow with the journey, without considering its purpose or goal. Trust your deep-rooted impulse to awaken and allow it to express itself. The journey itself will be exhilarating enough.

GUIDELINE 3: EVERYDAY LIFE IS PART OF THE ADVENTURE

Many spiritual traditions recommend leaving the ordinary world behind in order to focus on spiritual development. Some spiritual explorers take vows of celibacy and voluntary poverty and live apart from society, in monasteries, the forest, or the desert, meditating and praying in solitude.

It's easy to see the logic of this approach: of course it's easier to meditate if you're free of the stress of a city and the demands of family life and career. However, if we live as monks, we run the risk that our development may be lopsided and fragile, easily disturbed once we encounter the complexity and messiness of human society. In my view, it's more beneficial to incorporate spirituality into everyday life, which leads to more-integrated and deep-rooted development.

In any case, everyday life provides many excellent opportunities for spiritual growth that a monastery cannot. As we will see over the following chapters, we can gain significant spiritual growth through our relationships, our daily tasks and experiences, and even the challenges and crises of life. Our commonplace experiences and encounters offer myriad opportunities to practice presence, gratitude, acceptance, altruism, and other spiritual qualities. The world itself should be our monastery, and daily life should be our spiritual practice.

People are sometimes doubtful about whether it's possible to sustain a state of wakefulness while living an ordinary life in the world. If we were in a constant state of oneness and bliss, how would we deal with the practicalities of our lives, like earning a living, doing chores, and socializing?

However, awakening doesn't mean losing the ability to focus our attention and think logically and practically. When necessary, we're still able to concentrate and deal with everyday tasks. In those moments, feelings of oneness and bliss may fade into the background. But as soon as the tasks are done, we can relax our attention and reattune to our essential state. The spiritual qualities are always there as an undercurrent, below our surface mental activity.

GUIDELINE 4: BE FLEXIBLE

From the next chapter onward, we will cultivate certain qualities associated with wakefulness. However, it's important to note that I'm not presenting a sequential journey. The Hindu path of yoga (as developed by the ancient sage Patanjali) puts forward a step-by-step guide to enlightenment. It begins with ethical guidelines, moves on to yoga poses (asanas) and breathing exercises (pranayama), then progresses to concentration, meditation, and finally ecstatic union (samadhi). But in this book, I present an overarching, integral approach.

Disidentification from the thought mind is the most important initial step in awakening and so should be practiced first, which is why it's the first quality that we focus on. Aside from this, however, the book leaves a lot of room for flexibility. You don't necessarily have to follow the sequence of the chapters. Initially you might feel that you need to work on certain qualities more than others or before others. Later, you might feel that you're making less progress with some qualities than with others. Or specific life events — perhaps issues with relationships, your career, or your health — may cause you to focus your attention on particular qualities. So feel free to skip back to earlier chapters, repeating the exercises and meditations to reinforce those qualities. I encourage you to use your intuition.

Overall, the eight qualities we will explore in this book are equally important. Although you'll need to focus on them individually at first, eventually you should be able to integrate all of them into your life.

GUIDELINE 5:
THE QUALITIES ARE INTERDEPENDENT

One helpful aspect of the journey is that all the qualities are interdependent. As we cultivate each quality, the other qualities will naturally arise too, at least to an extent. For example, as you disidentify with the thought mind, you will naturally develop a greater capacity for presence, gratitude, and acceptance. And in developing presence, you will naturally disidentify from the thought mind. Similarly, as you cultivate a sense of gratitude, you will find yourself naturally developing more presence, and vice versa.

Because of this interdependence, you will find that the journey of awakening takes on its own momentum. Like a buoyant river, it will carry you along, even if you don't make a conscious effort to move. You simply need to stay afloat and let yourself be carried.

GUIDELINE 6:
HOW TO USE THE ACTIVITIES AND MEDITATIONS

Now let me offer you some more specific guidance on how to proceed through the practical exercises and meditations that form the core of this book. As with the chapters themselves, the book allows room for flexibility with the exercises and meditations. Don't feel obliged to practice all the exercises and meditations immediately (while reading the book) or in sequence. Certain activities and meditations may resonate with you more than others or may feel more appropriate at particular times. The exercises and meditations offered here form a wide-ranging palette of spiritual practices that you can draw from as required.

This book includes two main types of practical exercises:

contemplative exercises and *life practices*. The contemplative exercises are intended to expand your awareness and to encourage you to question ideas and aspects of life that you may be taking for granted. They include exercises to expand your empathy, to release psychological attachments, and to develop awareness of your mortality.

The life practices are exercises and guidelines to integrate into your daily life. They include techniques to keep you grounded in the present, to meet everyday experiences with acceptance, to cultivate gratitude, and to enhance your sense of connection to others. The book also includes some of my poetic reflections to illustrate the qualities of wakefulness. Most of these were previously published in my books *The Calm Center* and *The Clear Light*.

As we move through the book, the meditations will enable you to experience the eight qualities of wakefulness. However, you might wonder: How am I expected to read and meditate at the same time? I would suggest three possible approaches. The meditations are all quite short and simple, based on specific ideas or principles. So you could take a few minutes to read and digest the guidelines, then close your eyes and practice the meditations. It doesn't matter if you don't remember the exact wording, so long as you follow the basic principles.

Alternatively, you can follow the meditation instructions stage by stage, reading a sentence or two, then pausing. I have tried this process myself, and it works well. The reading of the instructions becomes part of the meditation process itself, and I enjoy the graceful movement back and forth between reading and the meditative state. Another possibility is simply to record the meditations on your phone and then listen to them with your eyes closed.

• *Ocean Meditation: From Discord to Harmony* •

Let's end this chapter — and begin the adventure of awakening — with a meditation.

Awakening is a journey from discord into harmony. The discord lies at the surface of our being, created by our restless thought minds. From there, it spreads into our daily lives, into our relationships, and into the world itself. However, underneath the discord lie the deep stillness and harmony of our true selves. Harmony is our essential nature. As we undergo awakening, we uncover this harmony by removing the conditions that obscure and obstruct it.

The following meditation illustrates this. It starts with a visualization.

Visualize the surface of an ocean. Picture the turbulent waves of the ocean, spraying and swelling. You can also hear the roar of the ocean.

Create an association between the surface of the ocean and the surface of your mind. The surface of your mind is just as restless and turbulent as the ocean, swelling and roaring with waves of thought. For a few moments, watch the waves of thought in your mind, just as you watched the waves of the ocean.

Now visualize the deep ocean beneath the turbulent surface. A few inches beneath the surface, and suddenly you're amid quietness and stillness. Way, way down, stretching for hundreds of feet below, you find depths of stillness, harmony, and peace.

Create an association between the deep stillness of the ocean and the depths of your inner being. Beneath the turbulent surface of your mind, endless depths of peace and harmony stretch way, way down. This is the essence of your being.

Let yourself fall beneath the surface of your mind and into that stillness. Find a space between thoughts and fall gently, like a diver, into the still, deep waters. Straightaway, you sense the harmony of your deep being. You can feel its calmness and quietness.

Let yourself fall deeper, knowing that you are completely safe in the stillness. Feel the harmony all around you growing stronger and more dense as you continue to dive deeper.

Looking up, you can see the surface of the ocean and the motion of the water. As you look, the motion slows and settles. Soon the surface of the ocean is calm and still, like a lake.

Next, let the image of the ocean fade from your mind. Now there is nothing but your empty inner space, free of images and associations.

And now there is no distinction between the depths and the surface of your being. There is just stillness, flowing through your whole being.

Let yourself float gently in the deep stillness of your being, like a diver in the deep ocean. Feel the stillness all around you, brushing against you, immersing you ...

Rest within the stillness for a minute or two.

Now return slowly to the surface of your mind, like a diver slowly rising to the surface of the ocean. As you emerge, sense the stillness of the surface of your mind and the stillness that stretches through endless depths inside you.

As we bring this meditation to a close, remember that the deep stillness of your being is always accessible to you. In your daily life, whenever your mind becomes turbulent, swelling with thoughts and emotions, you can always dive into deep stillness. You're always free to fall gently below the surface of your mind and into stillness. No matter how turbulent your mind becomes, the harmony of your deep being is always there, just below the surface of your mind, always close and always attainable.

As well as being a meditation in itself, this exercise symbolizes the entire journey of awakening. As we awaken, we gradually calm the surface of our minds and gain more access to the stillness of our deep being. We find that harmony is our most natural state and wonder why life seemed so difficult and discordant before. We feel a deep sense of ease, like a traveler who returns home after years of restless wandering. And in a real sense, awakening does mean returning home — to the harmony of our true nature and to the fundamental harmony of the world.

So let's return home.

2

DISIDENTIFICATION

Freedom from the Thought Mind

Close your eyes for a moment. You'll soon be aware of thoughts streaming through your mind — thoughts reminding you of the jobs you haven't done, anxiety about the future, fragments of memories, images of people you know, snatches of songs you've recently heard, and so on.

Now try to stop this stream of thought. See if you can experience a clear, empty mind, without impressions or associations arising.

It's unlikely that you will be able to do this. Involuntary thought chatter is an affliction of human beings. It's there whenever our minds aren't occupied with external things — when we're lying in bed trying to get to sleep or waiting at the bus stop or at the doctor's office. It's there when we do jobs or tasks that are too mundane to hold our attention. A supermarket cashier or warehouse packer may spend most of her day daydreaming about her next vacation. While caught in a mundane conversation with a work colleague, a man may find himself wondering what the weather will be like tomorrow or whether his favorite team will win their next match.

A QUIETER MIND

The minds of spiritually awakened people are less busy with thought chatter. Their inner being is spacious, rather than crowded with constant mental associations. This doesn't necessarily mean that they have no inner noise at all. Thoughts may disappear altogether, but this is quite rare. More commonly, thoughts become slower and quieter, fading into the background. Awakened people may also experience regular periods of pure consciousness, with no thoughts whatsoever.

For example, Eckhart Tolle told me that after his awakening, "My mind had slowed down. It was far less active. There were long periods in my daily life where there was no thinking or very little thinking or only important thinking. I was no longer identified with thought processes." Another awakened person described a background of "silence" inside his mind. He remarked that "because I notice the thoughts, because they are set against silence, they are not always there, and I no longer have the chatter endlessly."

At the same time, awakened people retain the *capacity* to think. It's important to remember that thinking is often useful. If we were unable to think at all, our lives would be extremely difficult. We often need to consciously deliberate in order to make plans and decisions, to organize our lives, to solve problems or contribute to discussions. Logical thought is the basis of philosophy and science. It's also helpful for us to consciously contemplate aspects of our lives and the world, in order to widen our sense of perspective and gain a clearer sense of our predicament. In fact, conscious contemplation can have an awareness-expanding effect and so contribute to awakening (as I hope you will find through the contemplative exercises in this book). At a deeper level, streams of thought can also be useful creatively, by generating ideas and insights. Creativity often arises from a deep level of associational thought, similar to daydreaming.

The important point is that we should be able to think *consciously*. We should be able to think when we need or want to. Thought should be a tool that we use — and enjoy using — as it is called for and then put down again. Otherwise, our minds should ideally be quiet.

Several years ago, I attended a meeting led by the English spiritual teacher Russel Williams, a highly awakened individual. One of the attendees asked Russel, "How often do you think? Or is your mind completely free of thoughts?"

Russel pondered for a moment. "I usually have about five thoughts a day. The rest of the time my mind is simply full of experience."

Of course, the next inevitable question was "What are those five thoughts?"

I was expecting Russel to describe momentous philosophical insights or pearls of spiritual wisdom. But instead, he responded, "First, I think about what I'm going to have for breakfast. Then, I think about what chores I need to do today. Later on, I think about what I'm going to have for lunch ..."

Even more significant than the fact that their minds are relatively quiet is that awakened individuals do not *identify* with their thoughts. In fact, this is the main reason *why* their minds are quiet. Awakened people know that they are not their thoughts. They know that the voice inside their head is not their true self. They can stand back and watch their thoughts from a distance, without being affected by them. It's as if they are sitting on a riverbank, watching a river flow by, without being carried away by it, with a wide space between them and the river.

Identification with the thought mind is the greatest single obstacle to spiritual awakening. And in the same way, disidentification with the thought mind is the most important initial step in awakening. Without this, it's very difficult, if not impossible, to take any other steps toward spiritual awakening. Disidentification with the thought mind is the gateway to awakening. And once we pass through the gateway, we never go back.

In this chapter, I will guide you through a process of disidentifying with the thought mind. I will also show how to disidentify with the stories that the thought mind carries about our lives.

THE ABSURDITY OF THOUGHT CHATTER

The first stage of disidentifying with thought chatter is to become aware of it.

In my early twenties, I decided to learn to meditate and joined a course at a local Buddhist center. At the end of the group meditation sessions, we had short individual meetings with the teacher, to check on our progress.

"So, Steve, how's the meditation going?" the teacher asked me one evening.

"Not very well," I replied. "Every time I sit down to meditate, my mind fills up with random thoughts about the future and past and absurd daydreams and scenarios about things that might happen. I find it really hard to concentrate. My attention keeps getting taken away by the thoughts."

To my surprise, the teacher nodded encouragingly. "That's good."

"Really? It doesn't feel good."

"What's good is that you're actually *aware* of the thoughts.

Most people are so identified with their thoughts they aren't even aware that they're there. But you can stand back and observe them, without identifying with them. So yes, you're making good progress!"

In fact, most people experience moments of disidentification from time to time, when they catch themselves thinking thoughts they don't like. You might be on an airplane, for example, imagining that the plane has a problem and is going to crash. You catch yourself thinking those thoughts and tell yourself, *Come on, this is ridiculous — stop thinking such absurd things.* Or you might be contemplating an upcoming presentation or job interview, imagining making a fool of yourself. For a moment, you step outside your thoughts and tell yourself, *Don't be so pessimistic — everything's going to be fine.* These moments are small glimpses of freedom from the thought mind. Unfortunately, most people quickly return to their habitual state of identification with their thoughts.

To become aware of thought chatter is to become aware of its absurdity. It's such a normal part of our experience that we take it for granted. But why should we have a kind of voice in our heads, a noise- and image-producing machine that jumps randomly from one association to the next? Doesn't it mean that we're all a little crazy?

Where does thought chatter come from? Perhaps it is a by-product of the ability to self-reflect — the ability to hold an inner dialogue with ourselves and to deliberate about and interpret our experience. Self-reflection can be very beneficial to us. But the ability often seems to malfunction. Like a computer that has developed a will of its own, the mechanism has somehow slipped out of our control. It interacts with other mental faculties, such as memory and imagination, to produce an endless, chaotic series of impressions and images. It is a psychological aberration, a quirk of the mind.

THE NEGATIVE EFFECTS OF THOUGHT CHATTER

Identifying with the thoughts that flow through our minds is the source of a massive amount of human suffering.

Firstly, thought chatter stops us being present. It takes us into the future and the past and into alternative realities. It creates a barrier between us and the world, a fog of abstraction that obscures our experience. At the most extreme level, we may become so deeply immersed in our thought chatter that we lose contact with reality altogether. The world of our thoughts becomes more real than the world outside our minds. At this point, we may be diagnosed with a psychological disorder.

Thought chatter also creates a disturbance inside us. Our minds contain a chaos of swirling thoughts that we have little or no control over. This makes us feel unsettled, in the same way as when we hear a loud disturbance outside. We have a background sense of unease inside our minds, as if something is not quite right, even though we can't pinpoint exactly what it is.

Another issue is that thought chatter triggers emotions and determines our moods. When we ponder unwanted future events, we switch into a negative mood, with feelings of anxiety and depression. If we ponder negative events from the past, it may trigger emotions like guilt or bitterness. Sometimes we think positive thoughts — say, about future events we're looking forward to — that might generate a positive mood. But the endless stream of shifting thoughts means that our moods and emotions constantly change. This creates a sense of restless confusion, as if we're watching a surreal film with a perpetually changing cast of characters and no coherent plot.

Finally, thought chatter centers our attention inside our mental space, confining our identity to our minds and bodies. It makes us feel that we are thinking entities who live *in here*, while the rest of the world is *out there*, on the other side. Thought chatter strengthens our sense of separateness by maintaining the thought mind as a distinct entity.

To disidentify with the thought mind means becoming free of all these issues. At the same time, it means stepping into the landscape of wakefulness and beginning to explore it.

Now let me guide you through some exercises to help you disidentify with the thought mind.

THE PROCESS

Thought chatter is simply a process that takes place inside our minds. Our bodies are full of physiological processes, such as the beating of our hearts, the circulation of our blood, and the digestion of our food. Thought chatter is just another type of process. Rather than taking place in our hearts or our blood vessels, it takes place in our heads. It's just something that our minds do, in the same way that our hearts beat.

We don't identify with breathing or digestion. We just allow the processes to take place, paying little or no attention to them. In the same way, there is no reason to identify with the process of thinking. We should just allow it take place, paying little attention to it.

You Are Not the Process

Sometimes it's demeaning to watch thoughts pass by
and realize how absurd they are.

It's like being sober at a drunken party
cringing as friends make fools of themselves.
"Can this really be me?" you ask yourself, ashamed.
"Is my mind really so full of nonsense?"

But whoever said these thoughts were yours?
Thinking is a process that takes place inside you
like digestion or the circulation of your blood.
And you are not your thoughts
any more than you are your digestion.

Pay as little attention to your thoughts
as you do to your circulating blood.
Take the contents of your thoughts as seriously
as the contents of your intestines.

Soon your thoughts will fade
into a background noise that doesn't disturb you
like the hum of a small television set, turned down low
flickering in a corner of a room.

And then you'll look inside yourself
and find nothing to be ashamed of.

Let me offer you two meditative exercises based on this principle. They are both quite short, no longer than a few minutes each. They take different approaches, so feel free to choose whichever one suits you best. The first, the Process Meditation, is a type of mindfulness exercise. The second one, the Riverbank Meditation, is primarily visual, so it might appeal to more visually minded people. Of course, you can also practice them both, sequentially.

• *The Process Meditation* •

Breathe slowly and deeply for a few moments, paying full attention to the process of breathing. Feel the air brushing the inside of your nose as you breathe in and out. Feel how your stomach rises and falls along with your breath. Do this for several breaths.

Sense how your whole being responds to the process of breathing. You can feel yourself becoming more relaxed as your breathing becomes slower, longer, and deeper.

Now bring your attention to the area of your heart. Be aware of its beating. Feel its pulse for a few seconds. Perhaps you can sense the pulse in different parts of your body — in the palm of your hand, for example.

Now bring your attention to another process, one connected to heart: the circulation of your blood. Feel the blood circulating through your body, through your veins, feeding your whole body with oxygen. Feel the blood flowing through your arms, down into your hands and fingers. Feel it flowing through your legs, down into your feet and toes. Feel it flowing up into your brain.

Now bring your attention to the process of digestion. Be aware of any food that might be inside your stomach, being slowly broken down and moving through your digestive system.

Be aware of those four processes at the same time: breathing, your heartbeat, the blood circulating through your body, and finally the process of digestion.

Now bring you awareness to another process: thinking. The four previous processes are connected to different parts of the body: breathing, to your lungs; your pulse, to your heart; circulation, to your veins; and digestion, to your stomach. In a similar way, the process of thinking is connected to your brain.

Bring your attention to your brain. Be aware of any thoughts, associations, and memories passing through your mental space. Watch them arise, as if you're watching a film. Allow them to arise, to take form, then pass away.

Observe the thinking process in the same way that you observed the other processes, aware of the distance between you and your thoughts.

Just as you don't identify with your breathing or blood circulation, you don't have to identify with your thoughts. You can just allow thinking to take place in the same way that you allow breathing or digestion to take place. Let the thinking process pass by without attaching yourself to it.

Why would you attach yourself to the process of breathing or of your heart beating? Similarly, why would you attach yourself to the process of thinking?

Finally, be aware of all five processes taking place inside you right now: breathing, your heartbeat, the circulation of blood, digestion, and also thinking.

Be aware of yourself as the witness of these processes, observing and allowing them to take place without identifying with them.

When you are ready, return your attention to the sounds inside this room. Pay attention to the sounds outside the room. Slowly open your eyes as we bring this meditation to a close.

The most important aspect of this exercise is to afford thinking the same status as other physiological processes. There is nothing special about our thoughts. There is no reason why we should attach more importance to them than we do to our breathing or digestion. There is no reason why we should allow our thoughts to immerse us and let them dictate our moods and our lives.

The Riverbank Meditation

Here is a second exercise — beginning with a visualization — to help you disidentify from the thought mind. If you just completed the previous exercise, I recommend pausing for a few minutes before beginning this one. (Perhaps go for a cup of tea!)

Picture yourself sitting on the bank of a river on a warm summer's day. You can feel the sunlight on your face, its warmth and light against your skin. You can smell the fresh grass around you. A gentle, warm breeze brushes against your skin. You can hear birds singing and the voices of children playing in the distance. You feel relaxed, but also alert and attentive.

For a few moments, watch the river flowing before you. You can see the sunlight shining on the water, flashing and flickering. You can see the foaming of the water, its ripples and waves, as the current flows by. Occasionally a boat passes by — a rowboat, or a canoe or kayak — with one or two passengers.

As you watch the river flow by from that place of stillness on the riverbank, you're aware of the space between you and the water. You can feel a calm spaciousness within your being as you watch the flowing and foaming of the river, the water in motion while you are in a state of stillness.

Now, remaining in that place of stillness, allow the image of the river and the bank to fade away.

In place of the river, be aware of the stream of your mental associations flowing by — any thoughts about the past or future, any daydreams. Like the river, they are constantly in motion. Take the same perspective you did with the river: sit back in a place of stillness, letting the stream of associations flow by without attaching yourself to any of them. Be aware of the space between you and the stream. You are free to just sit and watch, without being carried away by the motion of your thoughts.

Remain in that place of stillness for a few minutes, watching the stream of associations flow by. From time to time, you might find yourself latching on to the thought stream and being carried away. If that happens, simply step out of the stream and return to the place of stillness. Be aware again of the space between you and the stream of thoughts. Remind yourself that you are the observer of your thoughts. Remember that you're free to sit back and watch your thoughts flow by, as if you're on the riverbank, watching the river.

You can integrate the above exercise into your daily life. Whenever your mind becomes restless and you find yourself immersed in its chatter, return to the riverbank. Close your eyes and rekindle the scene of you sitting on the riverbank on a warm summer's day, with the river flowing before you. Step outside the stream of thought and return to that place of inner stillness. Soon, without the fuel of your identification, your thoughts will slow down and dissipate, like clouds that break up in a blue summer sky. Soon your restless mind will settle, and you'll regain a sense of calm equilibrium.

STEPPING OUT OF YOUR STORY

Now let's look at disidentification from a slightly wider perspective.

As well as producing thought chatter, the thought mind contains deep-rooted concepts about ourselves and our lives. These thread together to create a story of our life, based on our past experiences. We identify with the story, just as we do with our thoughts. We carry the story around with us almost all the time, at the back of our minds. The nature of our story helps to determine the tone and content of our thought chatter and our general mood.

We often reinforce the story by ruminating over it, recalling and reliving past events. In the case of positive stories, we reinforce them with physical reminders of the past. Perhaps you know someone whose walls are lined with framed certificates and photos, their mantelpieces with trophies and other mementos, all reminding them of their past achievements. Such people are trying to keep their stories alive, to maintain their sense of success and self-importance.

When we step into our stories, it strengthens our identity. This is why even negative stories can be seductive. Some people wallow in stories of failure and disappointment simply because it gives them a stronger sense of identity. (If they can blame others for their failures, even better, since they can further strengthen their identity by complaining and criticizing.) The frustration and bitterness of a negative story is preferable to the insecurity of a fragile sense of self.

So what is your story? Perhaps, as in the first example above, you carry a story of success and achievement. So long as you remember your story, you feel a sense of pride, thinking of yourself as an important person. Or perhaps your story is a negative one, full of failure, disappointment, and discord. As a result of carrying such a story, you feel inferior to others and lack confidence.

Negative and positive stories are both problematic. A negative story creates low self-esteem and a general sense of frustration and depression, with a feeling that you haven't achieved your potential and that the world has treated you badly. It also creates resentment toward others, whom you may blame for the events of your story. On the other hand, a positive story may bring exaggerated self-esteem, leading to overconfidence and arrogance. It may fuel a narcissistic sense of self-importance, a feeling that you're superior to others and deserve to be treated specially.

In a more general sense, our stories create a sense of *heaviness*. They fill our minds with conceptual baggage that weighs us down and saps our energy. We take this conceptual baggage into every situation we encounter, into every meeting with every person. It determines our responses, so that we don't react to situations spontaneously. Our minds are rooted in the past, so we can't meet the present on its own terms.

Let me illustrate this with an example from my own life. About ten years ago I completed a PhD in psychology. Naturally, my friends and relatives congratulated me, saying things like "What an amazing achievement! You should feel proud of yourself." I was grateful for their kind words but didn't really feel any sense of pride or achievement. I was just happy that the work was over and that I had a qualification that would allow me to retain my post at my university.

A few weeks later I attended the graduation ceremony with my family, including my parents. It was a bright summer's day, and it felt wonderful to share such a beautiful occasion with my loved ones. However, midway through the ceremony I started thinking about my past — how I had done badly at university the first time around, then spent several years unsure of my direction in life, drifting from one low-paid job to another, with periods of unemployment in between. It occurred to me that perhaps I *should* feel proud of myself. For a moment, I felt a sense of pride and achievement, while contemplating my present situation in relation to the past. As I did so, a heaviness arose in me. I felt the past intruding into the present, taking me away from the reality of this wonderful day with my family.

Somehow my pride tarnished the purity of the occasion. I

realized that the ceremony was beautiful and fulfilling in itself, without any story of achievement. So I decided I was going to leave the past to one side, to forget my story, and to give my whole attention to the present-tense reality of the event. In doing so, I felt a sense of lightness and freedom. I knew that my spontaneous present-centered joy was far more intense than any egoic self-satisfaction or self-esteem.

This experience made me aware that our stories are always potentially present, and we always have a choice about whether to step into them or not. I'm not saying that we should never feel any sense of achievement or never congratulate ourselves for attaining our goals. Of course, that's fine to an extent. But we should never gloat over our achievements to the point that they inflate our self-importance and take us away from the present.

This is the poem I wrote as a result of that experience.

The Story

Your story is always there
if you need to remind yourself of who you are
like a stream flowing beside you
that you can always step into and swim in for a while
whenever you lose direction or feel vulnerable
and need to refresh your sense of self.

And when you're flowing with that stream of memories
you might feel proud of how far you've come
to this moment of bright achievement
look back upstream and smile with vindication
at the fools who slighted and doubted you.

Or you might ache inside with failure
looking back at the meandering, muddy tracks
that have led to a place of pain.

You can be a hero or a villain, depending on your story.

Or you can let the stream flow by
and accept this moment in its wholeness
without reference to any other, before or after.

You can sit and observe, outside the story
not as a character but as the author
grounded in another identity
that was never created
and doesn't need a plot or conclusion
because it's already complete.

• CONTEMPLATIVE EXERCISE •
Stepping Out of Your Story

Be present to your physical experience. Feel the points of contact where your body touches the floor or your chair. Feel the points where your clothes touch your skin. Look around your room, taking in the reality of all the objects around you. Listen closely to any sounds inside the room and any sounds you can hear outside.

Then ask yourself: Where is my story right now? Where are my achievements? Where is my success or status? Where are my failures and losses? Where are my painful memories? Where are my ambitions for the future?

None are here. They are not part of the present, because they are unreal abstractions. All that exists right now is your experience of the present moment, independent of the past and future. Your story is just a mental construct. You can choose whether to bring it into the present moment or to leave it to one side.

So don't pick up your story. Let it recede into unreality. Step out of abstraction, wholly into experience. Step out of the past, wholly into the present. Let go of your story as you would let go of a dream when you know it's time to wake up.

True well-being doesn't stem from past achievements or future ambitions. Similarly, there is no reason why past experiences or anticipations of future experiences should create unhappiness in the present. Your well-being depends purely on how you feel in this moment. It depends purely on your inner state right now.

So let's consider: What is your inner state right now? In the absence of your story, in a state of presence, your inner state is one of natural well-being and wholeness. A well-being that doesn't depend on any concepts or memories or achievements or possessions. A well-being that stems entirely from presence.

In this state of natural well-being, there is no need to reinforce your identity. In presence, a deeper, more authentic identity reveals itself, self-sufficient and unconditioned. An identity that doesn't stem from your thought mind but from your essence, revealing itself when the thought mind is in abeyance.

While you retain this state of present wholeness, there is no need to step into your story. You'll be free to attend to every moment of your life without reference to your story, purely in terms of your present experience.

BEYOND THE THOUGHT MIND

As with all the qualities of wakefulness, disidentifying with the thought mind is a gradual process. You will probably pass through many stages between complete identification and complete disidentification. You may also find that the process is fitful. You'll no doubt go through some periods — a few hours or even a few days or weeks — when you feel relatively free of the thought mind, only to become immersed in it again. This might depend on the events of your life. In times of stress and challenge, it's easy to slip back into identification.

But don't be discouraged. It's inevitable that there will be some bumps in the road. The thought mind is very powerful, like a dictator who has taken complete control of your identity. Like all dictators, it doesn't relinquish power easily.

Identification is habitual. Like all habits, it has built up power over years and decades, gradually becoming stronger and stronger. But habits can quickly fade too, once we become conscious of them and override them with new patterns of behavior. The more often you step outside the thought mind, the weaker the habit of identification will grow. Eventually, it will become normal for you to let the thinking process flow by without latching on to it. It will become normal for you to rest in the bright clarity of the present moment, rather than to lose yourself in the fog of the thought mind.

As a result, you will feel a growing lightness and freedom, without the burden of your story. You will feel a deepening calmness, without the disturbance of incessant thought chatter. You will sense an inner spaciousness, without the clutter of thoughts and concepts. You'll also feel inner stability, now that your mood no longer shifts from moment to moment in response to the tone and content of your thoughts. The link between thought and feeling is broken. If any negative thoughts arise, they will pass away without tinging your mind with negative emotions. You'll be as steady as a rock on the ocean floor, rather than a cork floating aimlessly from wave to wave.

In addition, you will no longer feel separate. No longer rooted inside your mental space by thought chatter, you'll feel connected to your surroundings and to the world in general, as a participant, rather than an observer. And without your story bringing the past into the present, you'll be able to live more spontaneously, responding to situations and people in the moment, without reference to the past.

Perhaps most significantly of all, you will feel a new sense of identity. The seventeenth-century French philosopher René Descartes famously pronounced, "I think, therefore I am." The statement is usually taken to mean that the act of thinking generates our sense of identity and that without thought we would cease to exist. But strictly speaking, Descartes was talking about doubt. We can doubt everything — even that the sun will rise tomorrow morning — apart from our own existence as thinking beings. But so long as we think, we can be sure that we exist.

It seems impertinent to disagree with a revered philosopher who is unable to defend his ideas, but in my view, Descartes was wrong to associate identity solely with thought. We don't cease to exist when we stop thinking. On the contrary, we exist in a more authentic sense. The thought mind is not our true identity. It is a superficial self that obscures a deeper, truer being. As we disidentify with the thought mind, this deeper being reveals itself more powerfully, like the blue sky as clouds dissipate. This identity feels more expansive, stable, and deep-rooted. It is more essentially *you* — not a flimsy thought-created identity, but a state of pure, unconditioned being, as still and spacious as the sky.

3

GRATITUDE

Overcoming the Taking for Granted Syndrome

About twenty-five years ago, a friend told me about an amazing man who ran a local launderette. "He's like a guru! You have to go and see him! You might even want to write about him."

The next time my clothes needed washing, I went along to the launderette and met Tony, a tall, white-haired fellow in his late sixties. He told me about his dramatic transformation fifteen years earlier, after almost dying of a severe heart attack. Before then, he had been a successful businessman, working long hours and thinking of little else besides his job. But after his heart attack, his priorities completely changed. He felt as if scales had fallen away from his eyes and he could suddenly understand the meaning and value of life. As Tony told me:

> Happiness is being aware of how lucky you are to be alive, to be able to see the beauty of the world all around you at every moment. Do you ever stop and tell yourself how wonderful it is just to be able to see? Or how lucky you

> are to have this healthy body with two arms and two legs? Or how wonderful it is that you've got people around you who love you?

Whereas before Tony had barely paid any attention to his surroundings, now, in his words, "I feel like I'm living in a multicoloured world compared to a black and white one. Things seem so much more beautiful to me now." The people around him seemed so much more beautiful too. Prior to his heart attack, he spent little time with his children; now he phoned them every other day to tell them that he loved them.

After his heart attack, Tony sold his business and bought the launderette. He filled the walls with inspirational spiritual quotes, including, "I shall pass through this world but once. Any good therefore that I can do or any kindness that I can show to a human being, let me do it now." He loved to sit with the customers and share the story of his transformation. As he told me, "I love talking to young people especially. They're not aware of any of these things, they just take life for granted, so it's interesting to see how they react."

Tony also recommended some techniques to develop a sense of gratitude:

> What you should do is get up five minutes earlier than usual every day. And as soon as you get up you should go to your window, look at the sky and the trees and the sun, and say hello to them all — really say, "Hello tree, hello sun, hello sky" and so on. Remind yourself of how beautiful they are and how lucky you are to be able to see them. And there should be a moment in your day when you just think about all the people you love, your friends and your family, and remind yourself how special they are.

Tony had experienced a spiritual awakening, the main feature of which was a shift into a state of intense gratitude.

THE TAKING FOR GRANTED SYNDROME

We human beings have a strange blindness toward the blessings in our lives. Almost all the time, we fail to appreciate the value of our health, the people we love, our peace, freedom, and prosperity, and life itself. We often become aware of the value of these things when they're taken away — for example, when we become seriously ill, when our partner leaves us (perhaps *because* we were taking them for granted), or if we experience poverty or imprisonment. At that point, we tell ourselves, *If only I were healthy again — or if only my wife or husband came back to me, or if only I had money or were out of prison — then I would be happy again!* If the blessings return to us, we often do experience a honeymoon period of real gratitude and happiness. But this is usually only temporary. After a while, the taking for granted syndrome reactivates, switching us off to the value of our blessings.

The taking for granted syndrome is probably the result of adaptation, our tendency to get used to things once we have had them for a while. When we're first introduced to new experiences and environments — for example, the first few days in an unfamiliar foreign country, the first few days in a new job, or the first exposure to a new smell or taste — they affect us powerfully. But the experiences and sensations quickly lose their sensory power. We seem to have a psychological mechanism of desensitization that filters out the intensity of experiences, swiftly turning newness to familiarity. This is probably a way for our minds to conserve energy. It also makes it easier for us to focus on the practical tasks of our lives.

This desensitization may be helpful in terms of basic survival, but it has a massive downside: it means that we live in a state of constant discontent. It makes us feel that the conditions of our lives are unsatisfactory, so that we yearn for a different kind of life. It makes us want things we don't presently have, more of the things we already have, and less of other things we don't like. We live in a perpetual state of wanting, trying to alleviate our discontent by changing our life situation.

GRATITUDE IN WAKEFULNESS

One of the essential characteristics of awakened people is that they are free of the taking for granted syndrome. They never become habituated to the blessings in their lives, no matter how long these blessings have been present. They feel continually grateful for their bodies, their health, their family and friends, and their leisure time. They feel grateful for the food they eat, the clothes they wear, the homes they inhabit, and the trees, flowers, and other natural phenomena around them. They feel grateful for their freedom — their freedom to travel, to express their creativity, and to choose their own lifestyle.

Above all, awakened people feel grateful simply to be alive. They experience life itself as a blessing. They may have an intuition of some form of afterlife and so may not feel that this life and the world are all there is. Nevertheless, they feel that it's a massive gift and privilege to be alive in this form and in this world. They savor life as a fragile, temporary, and precious experience.

Transcending the taking for granted syndrome brings curiosity and openness. Now that they no longer take life itself for granted, awakened people don't take *anything* for granted. They have an acute sense of wonder and awe. Phenomena that others consider mundane seem strange and even miraculous to them. This is why awakened people often begin sentences with phrases like "Isn't it amazing that...?" and "Isn't it strange that...?" They're astounded by the beauty and strangeness of processes like childbirth, death, healing, sleep, and sex. They're awestruck by natural occurrences like the rising of the sun in the morning, the motion of waves on the ocean, the flight of birds, and clouds foaming across the sky. They gaze at the stars on a clear night and are amazed to be here, on the surface of a planet amid endless space, staring at astronomical objects millions of light years away.

To awakened people, the world never becomes familiar. Everyday experiences never lose their freshness and beauty. No matter how many times they repeat the same experiences — smell a flower, swim in the ocean, walk in the local park, play with their children, make love to their partner — they never get used to them.

As Tony's story illustrates, a shift from taking-for-granted-ness to ongoing gratitude is one of the clearest ways in which awakening manifests itself. Another example from my research is Eve, who underwent an awakening after many years of alcoholism. She told me that now, "I just feel light. I feel full of gratitude.... I live a simple, quiet life. I notice the small things, and I really appreciate them." Similarly, a woman called Cathy who underwent an awakening after a diagnosis of breast cancer described how she felt "real gratitude for the birds visiting my garden, the rays of sunshine streaming through trees."

• *Meditation: The Gift* •

How can we free ourselves from the taking for granted syndrome and cultivate ongoing gratitude? Let's begin with a short poem, then we'll do a meditative exercise based on the poem.

The Gift

As you breathe, inhale deeply
in gratitude for the gift of air.

As you eat, swallow slowly
in gratitude for the gift of food.

As you see, look attentively
in gratitude for the wonder of the world.

As you love, be passionate
in gratitude for the beauty of flesh and form.

As you live, be authentic and fearless
in gratitude for the gift of life.

Let's go through this poem again, and this time I'll guide you through meditative exercises related to the different verses.

As you breathe, inhale deeply
in gratitude for the gift of air.

Breathe slowly and attentively, aware of the sustenance the air is giving you. Remind yourself that the air is keeping you alive, providing your body with nitrogen and oxygen. Each time you inhale, feel the air refreshing and enriching you, filling your body with energy and life. As you exhale, breathe out gratitude to the air.

Breathe in the gift of air, then breathe out gratitude for the gift. Do that for several more breaths.

As you eat, swallow slowly
in gratitude for the gift of food.

If you are at home, near your kitchen, fetch a small piece of food, such as a piece of fruit. Or simply wait until the next time you sit down for a meal.

Eat each mouthful of food slowly and attentively, aware of its flavor and texture. Remind yourself that this food has grown from the earth. The food may also have been cultivated, picked, transported, and/or prepared by other people. Be grateful to the earth for providing you with this sustenance and to the people who helped to deliver the food to you. Be aware that each piece of food is sustaining your life, like the air. Each piece of food replenishes you, helping to keep you alive, healthy, and conscious. As you swallow each piece of food, allow gratitude to fill you.

As you see, look attentively
in gratitude for the wonder of the world.

Look outside your window: perhaps you can see the sky, some trees, houses, or other buildings. Pay full attention to everything you see, taking the time to observe shapes and colors and movement. Feel gratitude for this beautiful, intricate physical world of phenomena and forms.

Then turn your attention inside your room. Slowly observe the objects around you, absorbing their reality, their shapes and colors and forms. Feel gratitude for their presence and for the functions they fulfill.

As you love, be passionate
in gratitude for the beauty of flesh and form.

The next time you meet friends, relatives, or other loved ones, greet them with a sense of gratitude for their love and support and companionship. Be aware of their love and respect for you. Be aware of the long history that connects you with them — the challenges you have overcome together, the adventures you have undergone, the joys and sorrows you have shared. Be aware of the precious beauty of that person and how fortunate you are to share your life with them.

As you live, be authentic and fearless
in gratitude for the gift of life.

At this moment, while you're alive, be aware of the preciousness of your existence. Be aware that life is temporary and fragile, dependent on the healthy functioning of your body. The gift of your life in this form and in this world can be taken away at any moment. And it will be taken away eventually. So be grateful for your life while you have it.

And while this gift is yours, live authentically, without fear. Life is such a great privilege that you can't afford to waste it procrastinating, refusing opportunities, conforming to other people's desires, or following society's conventions. Life is so precious that it demands to be lived fully and fearlessly.

THE GRATITUDE OF ASTRONAUTS

In the late 1960s and early 1970s, twenty-four American astronauts traveled to the moon. As they gazed at the Earth from space, several had spiritual experiences that permanently transformed them. For example, Gene Cernan, a member of the Apollo 10 and 17 missions, saw the Earth as "dynamic, overwhelming... there was too much purpose, too much logic. It was too beautiful to happen by accident.... There has to be a creator of the universe who stands above the religions that we ourselves create to go on in our lives." Similarly, Edgar Mitchell, a member of the third successful mission to the moon, in January 1971, felt an overpowering sense of peace and tranquility, which he later described as "interconnected euphoria" and "instant global consciousness."

One of the most significant aspects of the astronauts' experiences was a tremendous sense of gratitude. They were aware that everything that they loved and gave their lives meaning was *there*, on the surface of that tiny globe. Rusty Schweickart was a member of the Apollo 9 mission, which carried out tests in March 1969 to prepare for the moon landings later that year. As he poetically described his experience, "You realize that on that small spot, that little blue and white planet, is everything that means anything to you — all of the history and music and poetry and art and death and birth and love, tears, joys, games, all of it on that little spot out there.... This tiny beautiful earth — the planet that keeps us alive, which gives us everything we have, the food we eat, the water we drink, the air we breathe, the beauty of nature."

Alan Bean, the fourth person to walk on the moon, felt a similar sense of wonder and gratitude that remained with him for the rest of his life. In a documentary forty years later, he remarked, "Since that time I have not complained about the weather a single time. I'm glad there *is* weather. I've not complained about traffic — I'm glad there's people around." Bean recalled that after his return from the moon, he used to go to shopping malls and sit down to watch people walking by, thinking, "Boy, we're lucky to be here. Why do people complain about the Earth? We are living in the Garden of Eden!"

• CONTEMPLATIVE EXERCISE •
Traveling to the Moon

Let me take you on a journey — in fact, the same journey that the astronauts took.

Close your eyes. Remind yourself that you're sitting (or standing) on the surface of the planet Earth, a globe approximately eight thousand miles in diameter. Be aware of the Earth underneath you, the thin layers of soil with deep layers of solid rock beneath, stretching down to the planet's molten core. Be aware of the space around you, filling your surroundings — the sky and the whole of the Earth's atmosphere. Be aware of the space spreading further, beyond the Earth's atmosphere. Sense the lack of boundary between the space around you and the space that fills the solar system and the universe. It is the same space.

Also be aware of the billions of other humans who share the Earth with you, distributed over bodies of land between the great oceans that fill most of the planet's surface. Also become aware of the millions of different species who share this planet with us, innumerable varieties of life-forms inhabiting every kind of environment and climate.

Now imagine yourself leaving the surface of the Earth, perhaps in a spaceship, an air balloon, or simply by yourself, as if you've become weightless or are having an out-of-body experience. Picture yourself rising above your town, into the clouds, above the hills and mountains, above the oceans, into the Earth's atmosphere, and beyond it, into space.

You continue to rise through space, feeling safe and relaxed, enjoying the freedom of flight. Looking below, you see the Earth receding, the contours of mountains and the masses of clouds growing more faint. The Earth's spherical shape slowly reveals itself.

Looking ahead, you see the moon, where you're headed, growing larger, revealing more detail as you approach. Its silver light glows more brightly. Its craters become more defined.

Soon you touch down on the moon. Although it's beautiful, you're struck by how barren and inhospitable it seems. You're also surprised by the emptiness and blackness of the space around you. The sheer endlessness of the space, seemingly stretching forever through the universe, shocks you.

Now you turn and look back at the Earth, this small, shining blue pearl in the middle of endless, empty darkness, a beautiful, bright oasis in the desert of space. You realize that everything that constitutes your life, everything you know and love, is there, on the surface of this small, fragile planet.

Contemplate your life, the life that takes place on the surface of that planet. Which aspects of your life seem most precious to you? Which people do you miss most, from two hundred thousand miles away? What will you most appreciate when you return to Earth?

Also consider which aspects of the planet itself seem most treasured and beautiful to you. Do you long to swim in the ocean, hike in the mountains, or walk in the woods? Do you yearn to feel light rain on your face or a gentle breeze against your skin?

Now let's return to the Earth. Hold all these beautiful and precious aspects of life in your heart as you bring your attention back to your surroundings. Reorient yourself in your room, feeling the chair or floor that you're sitting on and your feet against the hard ground. Listen to the sounds inside and outside your room. Slowly open your eyes, still full of gratitude for the miracle of life on Earth.

• LIFE PRACTICE •
An Appreciation List

Let's work with the intense gratitude that we're experiencing now.

To a large extent — as with our tendency to identify with the thought mind — our tendency to take things for granted is a habit. It's a kind of forgetfulness. We simply switch off our attention to our blessings and forget that they are all around us. As noted above, sometimes we rekindle awareness of blessings when they are removed, such as when we become ill or when a relationship ends. Another situation that can trigger awareness of our blessings is when we encounter other people who lack them. For example, we may be reminded of the value of our health when we meet people who are seriously ill. Or we may recall the value of our peace and prosperity if we visit countries that are afflicted by war and poverty.

In such situations, we're simply being reminded of what we already know, like a concussed person who is prompted by a medic to remember who and where she is. But why should we wait for other people to rekindle awareness of our blessings? We can also practice what I call *self-reminding.*

The following exercise is a simple way to remind yourself of your blessings and cultivate an ongoing awareness of them.

Following your journey to the moon, take a sheet of paper and write down the aspects of your life that seemed most precious when you gazed at the Earth. You could write sentences beginning with the words "I feel grateful for..." or "I am fortunate because..." or "I'm glad I'm..."

Write as many sentences as you can. When you have several (perhaps seven or eight), create a poster of the sentences that you can pin to the wall, in a place that you regularly walk by — perhaps your kitchen, hallway, or bathroom. If you like, set certain times of the day to read and contemplate the items — once in the morning and once before going to bed, for example. Or, less formally, simply stop for a few minutes once or twice a day when you pass the list, to read through the items and digest their meaning.

According to psychologists, new habits become ingrained after several weeks of conscious practice. So after several weeks of self-reminding, an attitude of gratitude should become normal and natural to you, overriding the taking for granted syndrome. It will become normal to feel grateful for your health, your beautiful friends and relatives, your freedom and prosperity, and the wonder and beauty of the natural world. It will become normal to feel gratitude for the simple fact that you are alive and conscious. Life in and of itself will become a gift and a privilege.

THE EFFECTS OF GRATITUDE

As you transcend the taking for granted syndrome, gratitude will bring major changes to your life. At my university, I teach a module on positive psychology, which is essentially the study of human well-being. Positive psychologists believe that gratitude is the most essential component of happiness, since it has such powerful effects, spreading into every area of our lives. It makes us more optimistic, enthusiastic, and confident. It makes us more resilient in the face of challenges and less prone to negative states like boredom and anxiety. It enhances our relationships and our physical health too.

Perhaps the most notable overall change, though, is a general sense of well-being. In the same way that the taking for granted syndrome inevitably leads to frustration and dissatisfaction, ongoing gratitude leads to contentment and fulfillment. You will no longer crave things you don't have or need, since you're now able to appreciate what you do have. You'll be free of the constant niggling need to add more to your life or to change your life situation, like an addict who is finally free of the craving for drugs.

You will also feel an enhanced sense of presence. In chapter 1, I mentioned that many qualities of wakefulness are interdependent, and this is particularly true of presence and gratitude. Gratitude brings us into presence, and presence creates gratitude. Our blessings are always in the present, whereas the taking for granted syndrome takes us out of the present, into imaginary future scenarios.

You might wonder: Is it actually *possible* to live in an all-encompassing state of gratitude, continually aware of the myriad blessings in our lives? But we don't have to extend our gratitude so widely all the time. The most important thing is to direct gratitude toward the experiences we are having at any particular moment. When eating, we should be grateful for food; when exercising, we should feel grateful for our bodies; when sharing our friends' company, we should be grateful for them; when walking through the countryside, we should feel grateful for the beauty around us; and so on. Gratitude should be a constant, underlying trait that arises organically in relation to our experience. And when we do have free moments of contemplation, we will naturally find ourselves extending our gratitude more widely, to encompass all of life itself and the Earth.

We should also remember that, as suggested in chapter 1, it's unrealistic — and even unnecessary — to live in a perpetual state of spiritual ecstasy. Of course, we often have to focus our attention on practical tasks, such as driving or cooking or earning a living. In those practical moments, our sense of gratitude may recede from our awareness. But it will always be in the background, naturally arising when we relax our attention. This applies to all the other qualities of wakefulness in this book and to wakefulness in general.

WOULD YOU CHOOSE TO BE BORN?

I was once friendly with a work colleague who couldn't see the point in being alive. As far as I know, he didn't suffer from depression, but he held the standard Western scientific view that human beings are nothing more than biological machines and that life is a meaningless, random process. He believed that his consciousness was just the product of chemical activity in the brain and that life after death was impossible. My friend had a university degree, earned a fairly good salary, and liked to spend his free time reading, watching soccer, and going to pubs or concerts with friends. In spite of this, he felt that he was just passing the time, filling a meaningless space between birth and death.

"Let me ask you a question, Steve," he said to me one day over a drink in a pub. "Now that you know what life is like, would you have chosen to be born?"

"Definitely!" I replied instantly. "Wouldn't you?"

He shook his head firmly, seeming surprised by my enthusiastic response. "No! Why would I willingly put myself through all this? All this boredom and monotony. All this frustration and anxiety. Not to mention illness, old age, and death at the end of it. Who would choose all of that?"

To him, it seemed perfectly self-evident that life is meaningless. He reminded me of existentialist philosophers such Jean-Paul Sartre and Albert Camus, who discussed the absurdity and futility of human life. There is even a modern philosophy called "antinatalism" whose premise is that it is better not to be born. Parents wrong their children by bringing them into the world, the thinking goes, by exposing them to the sufferings of life, which easily outweigh its positive aspects.

However, the issue with such philosophers — and my friend — is that they believe they are evaluating life objectively when in fact they're simply looking through the prism of their own minds, through psychological processes and structures that determine their outlook. They're like people who have a visual impairment without realizing it and assume that the hazy dullness around them is the true nature of things. In particular, this bleak philosophical outlook describes reality as it appears through the taking for granted syndrome, which switches off our attention to the beauty and wonder of life. In addition, the outlook stems from an aberrational state of duality, created by strong ego boundaries that cause a sense of separation. This brings a feeling of disconnection and alienation from the world.

A year or so later, I was walking through the center of my town on a beautiful autumn morning. The sunlight was so incandescent and the sky was so perfectly blue that I felt ecstatic. Remembering the conversation with my friend, I told myself that yes, I would definitely have chosen to be born. Moments of beauty and ecstasy such as this meant that life itself was a magnificent blessing.

Later that day, I wrote a poem in answer to my friend.

I Am Eternally Grateful

"Now that you know what life is like
would you have chosen to be born?"
a pessimistic friend once asked.
He seemed surprised when I replied, "Of course!"

I ponder the question again this morning —
this ecstatic autumn morning
that fills me with right-ness and yes-ness
this morning of brilliant astral sunlight
that makes the whole world seem transparent
and this blue-beyond-perfection sky
that shimmers with radiant stillness
and pure white clouds that foam and merge
nuzzling like new spring lambs.

Yes, I am grateful to have been born.
I am eternally grateful
for the gift of this brief life
to be a guest of time and space
hosted by this bountiful beautiful world
to taste the sweetness of substance
and the firmness of form and flesh.

I am eternally grateful
to be eternal
to never have been born
and to never die.

• *Gratitude Meditation* •

Let's conclude this chapter with a general meditation on gratitude. Don't feel that you have to practice this meditation now. It is a useful way of summarizing the different blessings of our lives. You can use it whenever your sense of gratitude needs to be reinforced.

If you do practice the meditation in the same sitting as the previous exercises, feel free to skip the first part (recalling an act of kindness), since you should already feel a warm glow of gratitude inside you.

Recall a situation when a person showed you kindness and you were filled with gratitude. Take a few moments to allow such an occasion to come to mind.

Replay the situation and allow the feeling of gratitude to fill you again now. You can feel it as a warm glow in the area of your heart. As you focus on the feeling, it intensifies, as if glowing more brightly.

Allow the situation to fade from your mind, but retain the sense of gratitude. Let it fill the whole of your awareness, as if you are nothing but a carrier of pure, radiant gratitude.

Now we're going to work with the warm glow of gratitude, spreading it to different aspects of your life.

Let's begin with your body. Consider your vital organs and the work they are doing inside you right now to keep you healthy and alive and conscious. Extend the warm glow of gratitude to them — to your heart, your lungs, your kidneys, liver, and stomach. Consider your limbs and muscles and the flexibility and strength they give you. Extend the glow of gratitude to your shoulders and arms, down through your chest, and to your legs and feet. Feel the radiance of gratitude filling your whole body.

Now let's consider your mind. Contemplate the work your mind does to organize your life, to make decisions and plans, to solve problems, and to express your creativity. Be aware of the amazing service your mind provides, and extend the warm glow of gratitude to it.

Consider your senses, through which you experience the wonder of the world: the eyes that open your awareness to the beautiful faces of your friends and the sublime beauty of nature; the ears that open your awareness to conversation and music; the sense of taste that allows you to savor food and drink; the sense of smell that opens your awareness to the scent of flowers and food; the sense of touch that allows you to feel your lover's body, run your fingers through your children's hair, and stroke your pets. Be aware of these amazing gifts and extend the warm glow of gratitude to each of your senses.

Now let's move outside your body. Contemplate the people you love, your family and friends and other loved ones. Picture them, wherever they are in the world right now, in the midst of their daily lives. Extend the warm glow of gratitude toward them, for their love and friendship and support.

Be aware of the Earth, the planet whose surface you're living on, which provides you with food and offers you so much beauty. Feel the Earth beneath you, the layers of vegetation and soil and rock stretching deep below. Extend your warm glow of gratitude to this beautiful green oasis, to the natural world around you and the soil and rock beneath you.

Be aware of the Earth's atmosphere, the thin layer of air that separates us from space and enables us to survive on this planet in the midst of the universe. Spread your warm glow of gratitude into the atmosphere.

And beyond the atmosphere, be aware of the sun, the giant burning star ninety-three million miles away, on which all life on Earth depends. Contemplate how it provides us with heat and light, without which we would be unable to live for one second. Let your warm glow of gratitude spread beyond the Earth's atmosphere and across space toward the sun.

Now you can feel a warm glow of gratitude radiating everywhere around you, filling the whole of your body and mind and senses, spreading to all the people you love, the Earth, the atmosphere, and into space, reaching toward the sun. For a moment, rest within that all-encompassing glow of gratitude.

The essence of gratitude is love. Gratitude is simply love directed toward a specific person or phenomenon that provides us with support or service. So what you are experiencing now is love, shining from the essence of your being.

This love is not only your essence, but the essence of all things, and of reality itself. You can sense the essential love of your own being merging with the essential love of the universe itself. You can sense love as a radiant force, glowing through all space and all things.

Let's rest within this all-pervading love for a moment, feeling its radiance within our being and everywhere around us ...

Now sense the solidity of your body again. Feel the points of contact where your body meets your environment — where your feet meet the floor, your body meets the chair, and your clothes meet your skin.

As we bring this meditation to a close, let's make an intention to sustain this warm glow of gratitude, to direct it to every aspect of our lives and everyone we share our lives with.

4

PRESENCE

Freedom from Time

Human beings are probably the most inappropriately named species on our planet. Most of us spend very little time *being*. It would be more accurate to call us human *doings*, human *thinkings*, or perhaps human *wantings* — with *being* somewhere near the bottom of the list.

Most of us find it very difficult to *be* — to be inactive, or to do nothing — and so spend most of our time *doing*, filling every moment with activities and distractions. When we have nothing to focus our attention on, we usually feel uneasy and immediately reach for some means of occupying our minds, such as a computer, TV show, or magazine.

I grew up before the age of the internet, and in those days people's major leisure activity was watching television. In our family house, the TV was always on, from morning to night. As a teenager, I remember walking along a row of terraced houses near my home one summer evening. Through the windows of every single house, I could see the same scene: people sitting on the sofa, immobile and silent, watching television. It struck me as absurd. Why did they all have to do this? Why were they all in a trancelike state staring at picture boxes? Why couldn't they just *be* in their rooms, existing in the moment, sitting quietly with their attention unfocused, doing nothing in particular? Why did they have to immerse their attention in soap operas and game shows?

As I walked past the row of houses, I realized that all those people watching television in their living rooms were in a state of absence. They weren't really *there*. Rather than experiencing the sensory reality of life in the present, their attention was immersed in alternate fictional worlds.

Unfortunately, this is the customary state of most human beings, especially now that we have so many electronic devices and social media sites to occupy our attention. We are rarely present to our surroundings or our experience. Our bodies are always present, of course, occupying physical space and interacting with the environment. (This is why — as we will see later — bringing your attention into the body is such an effective way of cultivating presence.) But our minds are usually elsewhere, immersed in entertainments or activities or, failing that, in daydreams, memories, and other forms of mental chatter.

Most people's default state is an inner discord caused by the restless thought activity of their minds and a feeling of separation from the world. On sensing this discord, they have an immediate impulse to escape from it by occupying or distracting their minds. This is why television became such a popular form of entertainment from the 1950s onward. Watching TV is so hypnotically absorbing, and demands so little mental effort, that it is a perfect mode of distraction. (Of course, there's nothing wrong with TV in itself, if watched selectively and consciously.)

Presence equates to being. Being means that we are fully aware of our present-moment experience, including our surroundings and the sensations and perceptions we are having. Presence means being fully *here*, in the world, in our body and senses, right now.

PRESENCE AND WAKEFULNESS

Presence, or being, is an essential quality of wakefulness. Awakened people are centered in the present. Since they don't experience inner discord, they don't feel the impulse to escape the present and so spend much less time in a state of absence. Rather than finding presence a burden, they relish it. To awakened people, simply to be — to take in the reality of their surroundings and their experiences in the Now — is one of life's greatest delights.

This is why awakened people savor solitude and inactivity, which allow them to be present and to experience the simple joy of being. As one awakened person told me, "It's so nice just to sit and do nothing. That's one of my favorite times. I can just sit in silence for hours." Another person described how "I don't get bored anymore. I only work two days per week, and all I do otherwise is read books, go for walks, and meditate." Another person told me, "I can be on my own for long periods of time and doing nothing, and that is okay with me."

It's obviously necessary to contemplate the past and the future sometimes. We can learn from the past by considering our previous mistakes and achievements. We need to think about the future to make plans and achieve goals. However, the present should always be our main point of orientation. It should be the ground in which we are rooted, which we never leave, even when we contemplate other times.

In this chapter, we will make the present our main point of orientation.

THE THREE STATES, OR THE THREE A'S

We always have a choice to be present or absent, to be here or elsewhere. More often than not, we choose absence over presence. In most cases, this is simply an unconscious reflex — another habit, like the habit of identifying with the thought mind or of taking our blessings for granted.

I illustrate this with a concept that I call *the three states,* or *the three A's*. The three states are *abstraction*, *absorption*, and *awareness.* Through every day of our lives, we shift in and out of these states. At any given time, we are always in at least one of the states and sometimes in a combination.

Abstraction is when our attention is immersed in thought chatter. For example, while waiting at the supermarket checkout, a bus stop, or a train station, you may find yourself daydreaming or thinking about the past or the future. Lying in bed at night, your attention may become so immersed in thought chatter that you can't get to sleep. We tend to slip into abstraction whenever our attention isn't focused externally, because either we're inactive or an activity isn't interesting enough to hold our attention. Abstraction is our default mode, which we always return to.

Absorption is when we do immerse our attention in activities or distractions. If you have a job, you probably spend a good deal of your working day in absorption (unless the job is boring and undemanding, in which case you may spend most of your time in abstraction). Most people spend a great deal of their leisure time in absorption too, watching TV programs and films, interacting with friends on social media, or reading.

It's important to note that absorption is often a positive state. I make a distinction between active and passive absorption. The former is equivalent to what psychologists call *flow*, when we immerse our attention in stimulating activities, such as writing, painting, playing music or sports, or solving puzzles. In flow, we concentrate our minds and channel our mental energy, bringing well-being and vitality. Passive absorption is when our attention is absorbed without any mental effort, such as when we watch soap operas on TV or idly surf through videos on the internet. This doesn't involve any focus or energy and usually generates a sense of restlessness and mental flatness.

Awareness, the third state of being, is when we give our attention to our experiences and our surroundings in the present. It is equivalent to a state of mindfulness, in which the mind is *full* of experience, taking in the direct and immediate reality of the present. Awareness can be consciously practiced, but it also arises spontaneously, such as when we're walking in nature and our awareness is full of the beauty and grandeur of our surroundings. We often experience spontaneous mindfulness on vacation, when our awareness is full of the intense reality of an unfamiliar environment. It may arise after meditation or sex or when a crisis has abated, as our minds become quiet and still.

Absorption and awareness are sometimes confused with each other. The essential difference is that in absorption, our attention is narrowly focused, usually immersed in one particular activity, acting like a flashlight. In awareness, our attention is wide-ranging, open to whatever arises in the present, like a bright light in the middle of a room that illuminates the entire space.

Wherever we are, whatever we're doing, we can always choose our state of being. Whenever you eat a meal, do household chores, or walk to the shops, you can choose to do it in abstraction, absorption, or awareness. While you eat, you can choose to daydream, read the news, or be aware of the taste of your food. While you commute to work in the morning, you can choose to ponder last night's events, listen to a podcast, or be aware of the people and buildings around you and the experience of walking.

• CONTEMPLATIVE EXERCISE •

How Much Time Do You Spend in the Three A's?

Consider a typical day in your life. On average, how much time do you spend in each of the three A's? Think in terms of percentages: What percentage of your time do you spend in abstraction, in absorption, and in awareness? Take a minute or two to ponder this...

I've asked this question to hundreds of students and workshop participants over the years, and the results are fairly consistent. People report spending the largest amount of time (typically 60 to 75 percent) in absorption, the next highest (typically around 15 to 25 percent) in abstraction, and the lowest (typically 5 to 15 percent) in awareness.

The light of consciousness has a therapeutic power. Once you become conscious of an issue, you have already gone some way toward freeing yourself of it. For example, as soon as you acknowledge and accept that you have an addiction or an illness, you have already taken an important step toward recovery. In a similar way, the simple fact of recognizing (through the concept of the three A's) that we spend so much of our time in absence can help us cultivate presence. The essential change we need to make is clear: to decrease the amount of time we spend in abstraction and absorption and increase the amount of time we spend in awareness. In other words, we need to transfer our attention away from the first two A's and toward the third.

So as you live your daily life, observe yourself. From time to time, stop to check whether you are in a state of abstraction, absorption, or awareness. Just becoming conscious that you are in a state of absence — that is, in abstraction or passive absorption — is enough to create presence. As soon as you notice that you are absent, you become present.

• CONTEMPLATIVE EXERCISE •

Strategies to Avoid the Present

Another way to contemplate absence and presence — to shed still more conscious light on the issue — is to think about some of the strategies we utilize to escape the present. As mentioned above, most of us feel an instinct to escape the present because we experience an inner discord when our attention isn't occupied. So we're always looking for ways of escape, like addicts who are always seeking ways of getting high.

As I discuss these strategies, consider which ones you tend to utilize. In terms of the three A's, they are all variants of abstraction and absorption.

LATCHING ON TO DISTRACTIONS. *This is perhaps the most habitual and frequent strategy we use to escape the present. Picture yourself getting up in the morning and going to the kitchen for breakfast. You make yourself a bowl of cereal, and almost before you realize it, you turn on the radio, pick up your phone, or open a newspaper. Rather than paying attention to the taste of your cereal or to the morning scene outside your kitchen window, you latch on to distractions and immerse your attention in them. You have chosen to start your day in absorption rather than in awareness.*

We enact the above scenario dozens — if not hundreds — of times a day. While walking, we listen to podcasts or read text messages instead of paying attention to the buildings we pass or the sky above us. On the train, we read a newspaper or check our cellphones rather than looking at the scenery outside the window.

LOOKING FORWARD TO THE FUTURE. *Do you obsessively look forward to events weeks or even months in advance, thinking about* *them all the time, to the extent that it stops you from focusing on the present?*

There's nothing wrong with anticipating positive future events. If we're aware of some pleasant events ahead, why shouldn't we contemplate them and allow ourselves to feel cheerful? However, because we often feel dissatisfied in the present, we tend to take refuge in the future. We look forward as a strategy to avoid looking around at our present experience.

I once knew a woman who continually thought and talked about her next vacation. Months in advance, she would excitedly exclaim, "I can't wait to go to Spain! It's going to be fantastic!" Weeks ahead, she would buy clothes for the vacation and even start packing. On her return, however, she usually had a slight air of disappointment. Even though she claimed to have had a good time, it was obvious that the vacation hadn't lived up to her expectations. But it didn't matter, because almost straightaway she would begin to look forward to her next vacation, exclaiming, "I can't wait to go to the Bahamas!"

Many people do something similar with weekends, social events, concerts, weddings, or long-term goals and ambitions. In a mode of abstraction, they continually visualize these future events, growing more and more excited as the time draws close. Unfortunately, as with my acquaintance above, it usually means that they set their expectations too high, so that the actual events are disappointing.

Reliving the past. *Do you obsessively look back to the past, the same way that other people look forward to the future? Do you often find yourself dwelling on past events, to the extent that it stops you from experiencing present events?*

Again, there is nothing wrong with recalling the past. It only becomes a problem when we use it as a strategy for avoiding the present.

I've noted two variants of this strategy. The more positive variant is nostalgia, when we recall and replay pleasant past events. You may know some older people who are nostalgic not only for their own past experiences but also for the era of their youth, which they usually view more positively than the present, complaining about young people nowadays or about present-day entertainers or sports figures. Nostalgia can induce a pleasant mental state, but it usually has the side effect of making us feel dissatisfied with the present.

The more negative variant is when we dwell on painful past experiences. This type of thinking triggers guilt and regret, also inflaming bitterness and resentment toward people who wronged us. In turn, resentment creates grudges and can lead to aggression or violence if we attempt to take revenge for being wronged. Negative contemplation of the past is the origin of thought patterns such as "If only I had . . . ," "I should have . . . ," and "I could have . . . ," which are entirely futile and serve only to make us feel more dissatisfied.

UNNECESSARY ACTIVITY. *Do you find yourself doing things simply to fill empty spaces of time? Do you engage in household chores that don't really need to be done or work extra hours in your job because you don't know what to do with your leisure time? If so, you're using doing as an escape from being. You're trying to flee the present by immersing your attention in unnecessary tasks.*

There is a cultural aspect underlying this strategy. We're encouraged to be unnecessarily active by our modern materialistic culture, which teaches us that our lives have value only when they are busy and productive. We're taught that being equates to laziness, so that we often feel uncomfortable and guilty when we're inactive.

Rushing. *This is a variant of looking forward to the future, applied to activity. Of course, rushing is sometimes necessary in our hectic modern lives. But you may find yourself rushing even when you don't need to, when you have ample time to spare and no appointments or deadlines to meet.*

Rushing sometimes feels intoxicating. It can make us feel important, as if we're doing essential work, moving forward with goals to achieve. But when we rush, we are effectively rushing away from the present and into the future. By trying to reach the future as quickly as possible, we're essentially saying that we don't want to be where we are now — or to do what we're doing now.

Again, our predilection for rushing is partly cultural, due to the pressure to be active and productive. But as well as being antithetical to presence, rushing makes our actions less effective and efficient. It means that we carry out tasks carelessly, without due attention, which leads to errors. (As we'll see later, the exact reverse applies to slowness, which encourages presence.)

These five strategies are different ways of saying no to the present, of choosing to be elsewhere rather than here.

As with the three A's, once we become conscious of these strategies and recognize ourselves using them, we can begin to free ourselves from them. Observe yourself closely. When you feel the impulse to avoid the present — by latching on to distractions, looking forward, reliving the past, doing unnecessary things, or rushing — pause for a moment. Rather than immediately acting on the impulse, allow it to flow by. Remain in the present, in a state of awareness.

These strategies — like the tendency to be absent in general — are largely habitual. We've followed them so frequently for so long that they've built up a great deal of power. However, in the same way that we can override the taking for granted syndrome with a new habit of gratitude, we can override the impulse to escape the present with a new habit of presence.

• LIFE PRACTICE •

The Gentle Mental Nudge

Let me illustrate a simple strategy of cultivating presence through a poem. This describes a real situation when I shifted from a state of abstraction to awareness.

The Alchemy of Attention

When a mist of multiplying thoughts fills your mind —
associations spinning endlessly
images jostling and memories whirling
free-falling through your inner space —
you can always bring yourself back to now.

This morning, making breakfast for the kids
I catch myself daydreaming and with a gentle mental nudge
remind myself of where I am.

And straightaway the kitchen clutter
turns into spacious presence —
a mosaic of sunlit squares across the floor
fading and brightening with the passing clouds
the metal rims of stools firing sparks
steam curls floating over cups
reflecting silver spoons
the perfect stillness of spilled coffee grains

and the window smudges exposed by sun —
everything perfectly still and real
everything perfectly itself.

Attention is an alchemy
that turns dullness to beauty
and anxiety to ease.

The key phrase in this poem is "a gentle mental nudge." Whenever you catch yourself in a state of absence, employing one of the strategies described above, give yourself a gentle mental nudge back into the present, as the poem describes. It's similar to when a toddler walks along a path, gets distracted, and wanders off in a different direction. Then a parent gently picks them up and places them back on the path.

Reorientate yourself in the present. Refocus your attention on the objects around you and the phenomena you see outside your window. Be aware of the sensations you're experiencing right now — the feeling of your body sitting on the chair, the clothes against your skin, your body's tiredness or discomfort or warmth or cold.

As the poem describes, on returning to the present, you will be struck by the vividness and freshness of your surroundings. Objects and natural phenomena seem more powerfully real, more fascinating and beautiful. You weren't really seeing them before — or at best you were viewing them only through a haze of abstraction and absorption. In presence, the haze clears, and we perceive the world more directly and fully.

The more you practice the gentle mental nudge, the stronger the habit of presence will become. You'll find yourself less likely to wander away from the present, as an older child becomes able to walk in a straight line. You will spend proportionally less time in abstraction and absorption and more time in awareness.

Meditation: The SLOTMA Exercise

Our senses are openings — or doors, as Buddhism refers to them — through which we are aware of our surroundings. At any moment, streams of information flow through the different senses (visual, auditory, tactile, and so on), merging to create our overall awareness.

In the following exercise, we will work with the senses individually, isolating each stream of perception and switching from one to another. In doing so, we bring our full attention to our present-moment experience.

As a memory aid, I use the acronym *SLOTMA*, standing for "Smelling, Listening, Observing, Touching, Mentation, and All" (as in all the senses at the same time). I don't normally include taste because when I lead the exercise in workshops, we don't usually have access to food or drink. I also recommend practicing the exercise outdoors, in an active mode, which is difficult to combine with eating or drinking. But feel free to add taste if you do the exercise at home, where you could simply keep a drink or small amount of food by your side. (In that case, it would be the SLOTTMA exercise, with an extra *T* for taste.)

Note also that I include mentation, or thought activity, in the exercise. This isn't normally viewed as a sense, but it is another stream of information that flows into our awareness. (In fact, in Theravada Buddhism, there are six "doors of the senses," including the mind.)

Let's begin with the sense of smell. Close your eyes and bring your attention to your nose. Feel the breath entering and leaving your nostrils. As you breathe in, be aware of any aroma that enters. Hold your awareness there. Some smells may be pleasant, others unpleasant. Don't judge them — simply allow them to enter your awareness.

You may find that thoughts arise and pull you away into abstraction. If so, simply give yourself a gentle mental nudge back into your awareness of smell.

Now let's do the same with listening. Again with your eyes closed, bring the whole of your awareness into the sense of hearing. Be aware of the sounds inside your room, then the sounds outside. (If you're doing the exercise outdoors, simply be aware of all the sounds around you.) Some sounds may be pleasant, some unpleasant. Again, don't judge them — simply allow them to enter your awareness.

Once more, if you find that your attention wanders, give yourself a gentle mental nudge back into awareness.

Let's move on to sense of sight. Open your eyes and slowly look around, surveying your room or your surroundings. Let your vision gently range over the objects and natural phenomena around you, absorbing their reality. Let them enter your field of awareness. Don't attach names to them — just allow them to be as they are. If you're inside, look through your window. Notice the intricate details of any objects or natural phenomena you can see outside, with their minute variations of form and color and texture.

Now switch to the sense of touch or feeling. Bring your whole awareness to the sense of touch. Gently touch the objects around you, without attaching names to them. Feel their shape and texture, their roughness or smoothness. You can also do this with your skin. Feel the texture of your skin, on your arms and hands. Touch and feel your hair and your face. Also be aware of the points of contact where your body meets its environment — your feet against the floor, your body against the chair, the clothes touching your skin.

Now switch to your mind. Bring your awareness into your mental space. Observe your own mind in the same away as you did the other senses, watching thoughts as they arise, enter your awareness, pass through, and fade. Don't attach yourself to the thoughts — be aware of the distance between you and them. Remain aware of yourself as the observer of your thoughts, not as the thinker of them.

So we've been through the senses of smelling, listening, observing, touching, and mentation. Now let's be aware of all these aspects at the same time. Open your awareness to all of your experience right now, in every direction. Don't latch on to anything that enters your awareness — just allow it to arise and then pass away. Be aware of the different streams of perception combining and emerging through the different senses.

The great thing about the SLOTMA exercise is that you can do it anywhere. I love to practice it when I'm cycling, running, swimming, or walking in the countryside. You can also practice it in any situation when you're waiting, such as at the supermarket or subway or train station, when you would normally slip into a state of abstraction. It's an active meditation that you can always use to shift out of abstraction or absorption and into awareness.

CHILDHOOD PRESENCE

As you spend time in awareness, you may have an inkling that it seems familiar. It may remind you of an earlier phase of your life, when awareness was your normal state. I'm referring to childhood — in particular, early childhood, up to the age of eight or nine.

Some spiritual traditions have an ambivalent attitude toward children. Priests and monks are supposed to be celibate. Spiritual adepts are supposed to live apart from the normal world, meditating and praying in monasteries. Nothing is meant to divert us from our spiritual path — least of all a family, which takes up so much time and energy. In India, there is a tradition that spiritual development belongs to a later stage of life, roughly after the age of fifty. First comes the "householder" stage of raising our children and living a worldly life. It's only once our children are grown up that we turn our attention to the spiritual realm.

In some ways, these views make sense. Dirty diapers, a house full of screams and squeals, food-splattered walls, no time to read books or attend courses or retreats... isn't spiritual development just one of the many things we sacrifice when we have kids?

However, many parents find that, far from hindering it, raising children advances their spiritual development. Parenthood can itself be a spiritual path, encouraging qualities of wakefulness such as altruism and detachment. What could be more altruistic than devoting your life to the care of a tiny, helpless being, setting aside your own desires to tend to theirs? Equally, parenthood shifts our focus from our own lives to those of our children, weakening our attachment to life projects of ambition and success.

One of the greatest gifts of parenting is that it lets us share in the natural spirituality of children. Young children possess innate spiritual qualities that we recapture as we raise them. They have a natural energetic well-being; they are free from restless mental chatter; they don't experience a sense of separation from the world; they aren't psychologically attached to possessions or notions of success or status.

But above all, young children exist in a natural state of presence. In terms of the three A's, young children spend much more time in awareness than adults. The past and future barely exist to them. They don't worry about upcoming birthday parties or mull over that time a few weeks ago when another child disrespected them. They simply accept what each moment brings, without reference to any moments before or after. (By the way, this doesn't mean that children are enlightened in the normal sense of the term. As I explained in *The Leap*, there are significant differences between the natural wakefulness of children and the mature wakefulness of adults. I sometimes joke that young children are part enlightened beings and part narcissistic monsters!)

In this sense, children can be spiritual teachers. I certainly experienced this with my own children. They reminded me to slow down and pay attention to the isness and wonder of small things. If I was in a state of abstraction, they brought me back into awareness. While playing with them in the garden or the park, I gave myself wholly to joy and laughter in the present, forgetting to think about the future and past.

Once I was getting ready to go away for the weekend and said to my five-year-old son, "Are you going to miss me, Bill?" He looked at me with a puzzled expression and replied, "But you're here now!" It was a useful reminder to be present.

Young children's natural presence is linked to their heightened perception. They see the world as a fantastically vivid place, full of fascinating phenomena that adults consider mundane and barely notice. Unlike adults, children don't perceive the world through a veil of familiarity, filters of concepts, and labels of language. When they see a tree or an animal, they don't compare or categorize it. They perceive it directly and immediately, in its naked suchness, without reference to concepts or memories. But as we grow older, we lose touch with the naked suchness of things. We attach names and concepts to phenomena, and our perception becomes familiarized and automatic.

• *Meditation: Recapturing Childhood Presence* •

Let me guide you through an exercise to regain the natural presence and the fresh perception you experienced as a young child. This is an exercise in deautomatizing our perception and returning to the preconceptual, prelingual world of early childhood. We will bypass labels of language in order to perceive the isness of things.

Before we begin, I'd like you to have a small piece of food nearby, such as a raisin or nut, fruit, a sweet, or chocolate.

Close your eyes and bring your attention into your mental space. Feel the energy of your consciousness vibrating softly. If any thoughts are passing through your inner space, just acknowledge them and let them flow by. Sense the space beyond thought, where you can watch thoughts form and pass by without being carried away by them.

In that space beyond thought, there is an emptiness. A place without concepts or mental activity — simply a spacious emptiness. This is the essence of your being: pure consciousness without content. Rest there for a few moments. Feel the space growing deeper and wider. Enjoy the spacious emptiness of your inner being, filling you with calm well-being…

In a moment, we will return to early childhood. We will perceive our surroundings in the same fresh and vivid way as when we were four or five years old, without labels of language or concepts. We will bypass labels and concepts and experience phenomena as they are, in their isness…

Now open your eyes. Where are you? What is this strange room? What are these strange objects around you? Imagine you're seeing them all for the first time. Touch some of the objects closest to you. Imagine that you're touching them for the first time. Feel their shapes and textures.

You'll probably be aware of your mind's impulse to label the phenomena, to attach names to them. Let that impulse pass by, remaining aware of the pure suchness of things, prior to conceptualization.

Raise your hand with your palm facing you. Now we will forget the word hand. *This is a strange, five-tentacled appendage extending from your body.*

Examine it closely. So many wrinkles and tiny lines, crossing and intertwining. The closer you look, the more lines you see, as with looking at the night sky and seeing more and more stars. Look at the different contours, the inclines and synclines, flowing into one another. Beneath the surface, perhaps you can see a faint network of blue channels, also flowing and intersecting.

Feel the texture of this strange appendage. Turn it around. On the other side, the blue channels beneath the surface seem more pronounced. There is a faint covering of hair, which you can gently brush against. Look at the five tentacles, also covered with soft hair, wrinkled in the middle, with small, hard, shell-like coverings near their tips.

Again, notice your mind's impulse to conceptualize, to attach names to the different phenomena. Let this impulse pass by, keeping your attention immersed in the realm of suchness, of pure experience before mentation.

After a short while, you'll probably reach a point where the phenomena become strange and unfamiliar. They may even seem a little disconcerting in their strangeness. Now you're viewing them in a state of isness, beyond labels and concepts, just as young children do.

Next, do the same with the piece of food. Forget its name. Don't even think of it as food — just a substance or small piece of matter. Pick it up and look at it, examining its color and shape. Touch it for a moment, exploring its texture. Smell it for a moment, exploring its scent. What is this strange object, this piece of matter that you feel impelled to insert in your mouth?

Place it on your tongue, allowing any flavor to gradually release throughout your mouth. If there is no flavor, notice that too. Then slowly and gently bite into it, sensing how the flavor becomes more intense and spreads. Feel how the piece of matter breaks up into smaller pieces, disintegrating, and moves toward the back of your throat. Swallow it unhurriedly, savoring the flavor that lingers in your mouth.

Once the flavor has begun to fade, unfocus your attention, allowing it to widen to your surroundings again. Now let's bring this exercise to a close.

The realm of isness that children inhabit is always present, behind and beyond mental activity. It's simply covered with layers of conceptualization. The more time we spend in this realm, the more accessible it becomes. Eventually we will become adept at bypassing the mind's conceptualization process. It's simply a question of looking at our surroundings in a different way, learning to perceive the world purely and directly through our awareness, rather than through mental concepts. It's like a magic eye picture, where a 3D image is hidden inside a hazy two-dimensional pattern. It takes a while to learn the trick, but once you do, you can swiftly find any 3D image. With a quick adjustment to our perception, we're always free to enter the realm of isness, wherever we are and whatever we're doing.

PRESENCE IN RELATIONSHIPS

One area where presence is incredibly important — and where it can be fruitfully practiced — is in relationships. Often, we are not present to our partners, friends, or relatives, particularly if we have known them for a long time and so take their companionship for granted. For example, your partner might be trying to tell you about an issue she has at work, but rather than listening, you're daydreaming or thinking about your plans for tomorrow. You are in a state of abstraction rather than awareness. More brazenly, you might be in a state of partial absorption, listening to the radio in the background or watching television out of the corner of your eye.

A lack of presence brings discord into relationships. It makes friends and relatives feel disrespected. Even if we believe we're making a convincing show of presence — for example, by looking at our companion and nodding our head every now and then — they can always sense our absence, even if only subconsciously. Our absence tells them that we don't value them enough to offer them our attention. It tells them that we care more about our own thoughts or about the news on TV than we do about their well-being.

In the short term, this may give rise to arguments. In the long term, it may lead to the breakdown of a relationship. Presence is the basis of respect toward other people and the foundation of any harmonious relationship.

Without presence, it's impossible to form or maintain intimacy and affection. Abstraction creates a barrier, a mental fog that prevents us from understanding and empathizing with others. It stops us from recognizing their needs, so that we can't offer them the support they require. While our attention is focused inside our own minds or on our own needs, we can't truly connect with others. Our relationships are filled with misunderstanding and conflict rather than connection and harmony.

• LIFE PRACTICE •
Presence in Relationships

The next time a partner or close friend is talking to you at length — perhaps telling you why they feel angry or depressed or about something that has happened during their day — be conscious of your state in relation to the three A's.

If you are in abstraction, give yourself a gentle mental nudge back into awareness. Listen with full attention to what they are saying. Maintain eye contact. Remind yourself that everything they are expressing is significant.

As you're listening, erase your memory of this person. Imagine that this is the first time you've ever met. Forget their name. Look at their face as if it's the face of a stranger.

After a while, your perception shifts. The husk of familiarity falls away. You see the person as a real human being again, rather than a taken for granted part of your life.

Your companion will respond to your presence. They will feel valued. If they felt anger and frustration, this will fade away. If there was any discord in your relationship, it will fade away too.

In presence, you are no longer two isolated egos. A bond has formed between you — a bond of presence. Your beings have connected and begun to merge. Now you feel deep respect and love for each other, beyond familiarity.

As well as making relationships more harmonious, practicing presence toward your companions will help to build up an overall habit of awareness, which you can apply to every area of your life.

• LIFE PRACTICE •

Living Slowly

Let me recommend one final practice to encourage presence: slowness, or making a conscious attempt to live slowly.

There is a symbiotic relationship between slowness and presence, just as there is a relationship between rushing and absence. When we live in presence, we naturally live slowly. We walk more slowly, cook more slowly, do our chores more slowly, and so on. This doesn't mean we become any less productive or effective in our lives — on the contrary, slowness means that we're much more likely to make the right choices and decisions and to follow the right course of action.

At the same time, by making a conscious effort to live slowly, we naturally become more present. We have more time to pay attention to our surroundings and our experience. We have more time to absorb the reality of the flowing nowness of our lives. We flow with that nowness, rather than rushing ahead of it.

About fifteen years ago, I was working part-time at a college six miles from my home. I initially drove to work but found the journey stressful, due to heavy traffic. So I decided to start cycling instead. Because I could move freely through the traffic, the journey took only a few minutes longer than by car. It felt great to be exercising in the open air, rather than sitting stationary inside a car.

But the best thing about cycling was that it allowed me to absorb much more of the reality of the journey. I saw interesting old houses and beautiful trees and flowers that I hadn't noticed while driving. I saw turnings into small lanes and quiet avenues that I had simply bypassed in my car. Best of all, I could look at the sky, at the clouds and the still, blue spaces between them and the morning sunlight shining through. Every morning, I arrived at work full of positive energy. I was amazed at how much of the journey I had missed while driving, at how much more reality I sensed simply by traveling more slowly.

This a good analogy for life itself. We experience much more reality by living slowly, in presence. We also find life less stressful and more fulfilling.

In my book Out of the Darkness, *I told the story of Gill Hicks, an Australian woman who was seriously injured in a terrorist attack and lost her legs below the knee. On recovery, she felt like a different person living a new life. Because of her disability, she had to live much more slowly, which she saw as a marvelous gift. As she stated, "Being slow — physically moving at a slower pace — has been an extraordinary experience. I have seen so much more, just by being able to stop, look and absorb."*

Here is a poem that conveys the transformational effects of slowness:

SLOW DOWN

Slow down.
Don't be so desperate to reach the future
that you push the present away.

Treat each moment with respect
as a friend who deserves your attention.
Greet every new experience as a guest
who's welcome to be part of your life.

Slow down
and feel how the stress of doing
turns into ease of being.

Slow down
and feel how your rigid separateness
softens into spacious belonging.

Slow down
and see how the future fades like a mirage
and how the present arises around you
as clear and fresh as dawn.

LIVING IN AWARENESS

Living in awareness, or presence, means freedom and ease. It means freedom from the past and the future. We don't let past experiences or future anticipations define our attitudes or behavior. Rather than anticipating events, we simply allow them to arise and respond to them on their own terms. When we encounter people, we don't carry resentments and grudges from the past or intentions from the future — we meet them purely in presence.

When we live in abstraction, oriented toward the future and the past, our minds are restless with thought chatter. We feel the pressure of our life's demands and responsibilities. We feel anxiety from the future and guilt and bitterness from the past. But in awareness, this negativity disappears. Our minds become calm and clear, and life becomes simple. There is only the simple clarity of the present and the experiences that arise in it.

Another significant change that occurs in awareness — and another way in which life becomes easier — is that we no longer avoid inactivity and solitude. In the normal human state, solitude and inactivity are enemies, because they expose us to the restless discord of the thought mind. That's why people use the strategies of avoiding the present that I described earlier. Watching TV or keeping busy shields us from the unease of our minds when we are inactive and alone. But in awareness this is no longer necessary. We are able to *do nothing*, to live quietly in a mode of being. In fact, as I noted at the beginning of this chapter, awakened people *relish* solitude and inactivity, which allow them to feel deeply alive, connected to their own being and to the world.

In other words, in presence we become truly able to *live*, in a state of being, vividly aware of the beauty and isness of our experience. Life becomes so much easier and richer that it's as if we have awoken from an anxious dream into a beautiful, clear morning.

5

ALTRUISM

Giving to the World

One of the most significant changes that awakening brings is a shift from a lifestyle of *accumulation* to one of *contribution.*

In the normal human state, the main purpose of life is to accumulate. As separate egos trapped inside our mental space, we feel incomplete. Something seems to be missing, so we're always striving to *add to* ourselves, to compensate for our sense of lack. This is the root of materialism, the desire to accumulate possessions and wealth. In a more subtle form, it's the root of the desire for attention, power, success, and fame. Unconsciously, all this striving is an impulse to strengthen and expand our disconnected egos.

Unfortunately, the strategy doesn't work. While we experience separation, no amount of wealth or power or success can satisfy us. It's like trying to alleviate hunger by wearing extra layers of clothes. Unfortunately, many people never realize this. They believe that they haven't accumulated enough money or power and so keep striving for more. All the while, a sense of frustration builds up inside, as their goal continually eludes them. If they're fortunate, they may reach a point of disillusionment or even breakdown, when they realize that they've been following the wrong path to happiness. If they're especially lucky, they may gain the insight that happiness is an inner state, and start to heal their ego-separateness through meditation and other spiritual practices.

However, spiritually awakened people don't experience separation. They are not isolated egos, trapped inside their minds and bodies. They feel connected to the world and to other living beings, part of a shared network of being. As a result, they don't feel a need to accumulate. This is why most awakened people live simple, quiet lives, without too many possessions or too much activity. They don't feel the need to become rich or famous or powerful.

For awakened people, the main purpose of life is not to accumulate but to contribute. Rather than taking from the world, their main impulse is to *give* to the world. Their sense of connection creates a strong empathy toward other people and other living beings. They are sensitive to other people's pain and suffering, and so feel a powerful impulse to help others, to alleviate their suffering and enhance their development. In their daily lives, they act with kindness and consideration, supporting and serving their communities and treating others with respect.

Another important factor here is the wide-ranging conceptual awareness of awakened individuals. Their wide-angle vision of reality means that social or global issues concern them as much as, if not more than, personal issues. Coupled with their sense of empathy, this creates a strong urge to help the human race in general, to help solve social and global problems, to enhance people's lives through creativity or spiritual insight. Since they don't have a sense of group identity, this altruism isn't directed toward a specific country or ethnic or religious group, but to the whole human race, indiscriminately.

When people undergo sudden awakening, they often comment on this shift from accumulation to contribution. For example, Marcus had an awakening following a breakdown due to the stress of trying to become successful and famous. He described his awakening as "a shift in focus from what I can get from life to what I can give to life." A man who had an awakening because of the trauma of military combat told me, "The purpose of my life is to be here for others, to help them grow and see their own importance."

Because of this new altruistic orientation, many awakened people change careers, taking on less accumulative and more altruistic roles. After experiencing an awakening following a cancer diagnosis, Irene gave up her high-status role as an IT manager to retrain as a counselor and therapist. Gill Hicks, the terrorism victim whom I mentioned briefly at the end of the last chapter, gave up architecture and design to become a peace campaigner. In other cases, awakened people retain the same roles but change their attitude and approach. For example, LeeAnn had an awakening following the murder of a close friend. As a manager at a dermatology company, she shifted her focus away from profit and toward well-being. As she told me, "I want to make sure that every patient that walks through the door, every employee that works there, they're always respected, valued, cared about — it's ridiculously important to me."

SPIRITUAL ACTIVISM

Spiritual seekers are sometimes accused of narcissism, of caring so much about their inner well-being that they neglect social or political issues. Spirituality is sometimes associated with detachment and indifference, partly because of the monks and mystics who retreat from everyday life to further their personal spiritual development.

There are, it's true, some spiritual traditions that tell us that the material world is an illusion and spirit is the only reality. This view implies that all the problems that occur in the world — such as poverty, war, and environmental destruction — are also illusory, so we shouldn't be too concerned about them. A slight variant of this view is when spiritual teachers state that the world exists in a state of perfection and so problems cannot exist. Suffering may appear to exist but has a purpose in the great scheme of things. It's all part of a divine plan, or an overall harmony, and so we shouldn't try to interfere. Such attitudes certainly encourage an indifference to and detachment from the world.

However, in my research, most people who undergo awakening don't become detached or indifferent. Just the opposite: they become more concerned with social and global problems and the plight of other living beings. This is why there is such a long and rich tradition of spiritual activism by awakened individuals who work to bring about social and political change, often at great personal risk. Some famous examples include Florence Nightingale, Mahatma Gandhi, Archbishop Desmond Tutu, and Martin Luther King Jr.

Genuine spirituality manifests itself in empathy, compassion, and altruism. In one way or another, awakened individuals live lives of service. In one way or another, they all contribute to the welfare of humanity and bring healing to the world.

In addition to being one of the fruits of awakening, service is a spiritual practice in itself. Service helps us to transcend separateness. It softens our ego boundaries and connects us with others and with the world itself. It helps us to overcome our egoic desires, so that we become less self-centered. By giving to the world, we reduce our need to take from it.

In the rest of this chapter, I will guide you through some methods to practice service and enhance your connection to others. But before we begin, let me lead you through a contemplative exercise.

• CONTEMPLATIVE EXERCISE •

The Circle of Concern

How far does your circle of concern stretch? Are you concerned mainly with your own well-being, with satisfying your own needs and desires, without caring too much about other people's welfare? Perhaps your circle of concern also includes your family and close friends, so that you are willing to act with pure altruism toward them, offering them kindness without thought of recompense.

More widely, maybe your circle of concern stretches to your community or your religious or ethnic group. Perhaps you feel empathy toward those who share your beliefs and background but feel a relative lack of concern for others outside of your group. More widely still, maybe your circle of concern extends to your whole nation. You may feel that the interests of your country are paramount but feel indifferent to the issues faced by others around the world.

Or does your circle of concern extend to the whole human race, irrespective of ethnic or national differences? Do you feel a sense of kinship to all human beings in all countries? Do global issues seem as important as the issues that affect you personally or that affect your community or society? Do you feel a sense of mission to contribute to the well-being of the human race as a whole?

Or perhaps, even more widely, your circle of concern stretches beyond human beings, to the animal kingdom and other species. You may feel a kinship to all living beings, so that you do your utmost to avoid harming other species and feel a responsibility to protect their welfare. Along with this, maybe you feel empathy for the Earth itself, a kinship with the whole of the natural world, and a responsibility to minimize your own environmental impact, with a passionate desire to protect and sustain the Earth's ecosystems.

Or perhaps, most widely of all, your circle of concern extends to the whole universe. You may feel connected to a universal spiritual force or quality, which pervades the physical world but at the same time transcends it. Perhaps you feel an impulse to express and embody this quality, an impulse that directs the course of your life.

As we undergo awakening, our circle of concern grows wider and wider, from the personal to the communal to the global and, finally, the universal.

We can also contemplate this in terms of service. Consider the question: Who do you serve? Do you simply serve yourself, satisfying your own needs and following your own ambitions? Perhaps you serve your family too, by earning money or caring for your children or elderly parents. Or maybe, more widely, you serve your community or society, contributing through your job or through charity or voluntary work.

Beyond that, you might serve the whole human race generally, through environmental, social, or political activism, trying to alleviate some of the oppression and discord that fill our world. Or maybe you help the human race less directly, through your creativity or spirituality, spreading inspiration and wisdom.

You might feel that you are serving other species and the natural world too — the whole Earth — by living harmoniously and simply, helping to reduce environmental damage, or working with groups that try to protect the Earth.

Most widely of all, perhaps you feel as if you are serving life or the universe, by allowing a transpersonal force to express itself through you and to direct your actions.

As we undergo awakening, the range of our service grows wider and wider, from the personal to the communal to the global and universal.

CONNECTION

One reason why — as I suggested in chapter 1 — spiritual development shouldn't be divorced from everyday life is because everyday life offers ample opportunities for spiritual practice. This is especially true of altruism. Unlike monks who live in solitude, we have continual interactions with other people, which we can use to nurture our altruism and so further our spiritual growth.

I sometimes tell my students the story about the taxi passenger who made a whole town happy:

A man arrives at the train station and steps into a taxi for a short drive. He's friendly to the driver, asking him how long he's been on duty, if he has a family, and what he does in his free time.

As he pays his fare, he says to the driver, "Thanks for that. I enjoyed talking to you. And it was the safest I've felt in a car for a long time. You're a great driver." This puts the taxi driver in a good mood. He's then friendly to all his customers, which puts all of them in a good mood too. They're friendly to all the people they meet, which puts them in a good mood, so that they're friendly to everyone they meet… and so on, until the whole town is in a good mood.

From the opposite perspective, here is a story told to me by a person who attempted suicide by jumping off a bridge: He spent about half an hour on the edge of the bridge before jumping. During that time, a number of tourists and joggers went by without stopping or even seeming to notice him. He told me that if just one person had talked to him, he would not have jumped. To his mind, people's indifference (even if unintentional, since they simply may not have noticed him) confirmed that no one cared and made him determined to attempt suicide. (Fortunately, he survived the jump without serious injury.)

Both these stories illustrate the power of human interaction. Disrespect and indifference damage others. On the other hand, a short, friendly conversation — even a comment or gesture — can change a person's mood. It can restore their faith in human nature, lift them out of depression — even stop them from taking their own life.

Now let me recommend three life practices, simple exercises for creating connection that you can easily integrate into your daily life. It may well be that you already practice them, at least from time to time, or in a slightly different form.

• LIFE PRACTICE •

Give Respectful Attention to Everyone You Meet

As we go about our lives, working and shopping and traveling, we encounter dozens of people every day — colleagues, shopworkers, fellow passengers, waiters, bus or taxi drivers, unhoused people on the street, and so on. Often, we don't pay them real attention, because we are in a state of abstraction or absorption. We're too busy rushing or daydreaming or looking at our smartphones to smile or speak to or even look at them.

As a practice, do precisely the opposite. When you go in shops, offer your full attention to the person who serves you. At the supermarket, give your complete attention to the person at the checkout. Be aware of the service they're providing, the time and energy they devote to their role. Look them in the eye, smiling and expressing your gratitude.

Be similarly attentive with the taxi driver, the bank cashier, your neighbors, colleagues, and so on. If you offer money or food to an unhoused person, give them respectful attention. They may appreciate this even more than other people, since they're used to being disrespected and ignored.

Being attentive to others in this way — especially making eye contact — is a subtle but powerful form of altruism. It makes people feel that they are valued, that their role is worthwhile. It creates a connection that helps to transcend ego separation on both sides. As a spiritual practice, it's also a form of mindfulness that engenders presence.

• LIFE PRACTICE •

Radical Friendliness

As a young man, I spent a lot of time alone and had poor social skills. I was hopeless at small talk. When shopkeepers or bus drivers tried to chat about the weather or about last night's soccer match, I would shrug my shoulders and mutter, "I dunno." I was even ideologically opposed to small talk, because I thought it was inauthentic and trivial. Why can't people talk about important things? *I thought irately when I heard people chatting about the weather or TV programs.*

But now I'm the opposite. I delight in practicing what I call "radical friendliness." I love to chat with strangers, to make conversation with people on trains or on buses or while waiting in lines. A long time ago I realized the content of such conversations doesn't matter. They're simply about making a connection.

In this spirit, the second altruistic life practice I recommend is to form bonds of friendship with as many people as possible. If you're waiting in a line at a shop or train station, make a friendly remark to the person next to you. Start a conversation with your taxi driver, with the bus or airplane passenger sitting next to you, with the clerk or waiter who serves you. Practice radical friendliness without embarrassment or fear.

Here in England, people tend to be somewhat reserved and can be a little embarrassed about being overtly friendly. They're sometimes afraid of what reaction they might receive, as if people will say, "Leave me alone! Who do you think you are, speaking to me without permission?" But in my experience, no one ever takes umbrage; they always respond with cheerful friendliness. I can't recall anyone ever reacting with hostility.

Of course, some people may misinterpret your friendliness. They may initially be suspicious, thinking you're trying to sell them something or making romantic overtures. But if your attentions are genuinely altruistic, they will quickly sense this.

By practicing radical friendliness, you'll leave behind a network of connection at the end of every day. In a small but significant way, you will decrease otherness and hostility in the world, creating ripples of goodwill that will strengthen as they spread, as in the story of the taxi driver.

• LIFE PRACTICE •

Conscious Altruism

At my university, I teach a module on positive psychology, which includes a session on altruism. I begin the session by asking my students to recall a situation where they received an act of kindness and another situation where they performed an altruistic act.

I will ask the same of you now… Take a minute or so to think of two examples.

Consider the motivation of these two altruistic acts. Were they expressions of genuine kindness, or did they have some ulterior motive?

It's important to ask this question because many modern scientists and philosophers are skeptical about "pure" altruism. They believe that human beings are essentially selfish and that pure altruism — at least toward strangers — has no evolutionary basis. Why would we have evolved to put other people's well-being before our own, possibly even endangering our chances of survival? So there must be some hidden selfish motive to altruism, such as impressing other people, improving our chances of having sex, feeling good about ourselves, ensuring that we receive favors in return, and so on.

There may indeed be ulterior motives behind some acts of altruism. But after you ponder your two altruistic acts — and your life in general — I think you would agree that pure altruism does exist and is actually common. Human beings do frequently offer kindness to strangers without any thought of benefit. Pure altruism is the result of empathy, which allows us to sense other people's suffering. This triggers an impulse to relieve their suffering, just as when we feel an impulse to alleviate our own personal pain. Altruism is natural to human beings because we are naturally empathic.

At the end of the altruism class, I give my students some homework: I ask them to perform as many acts of kindness as they can over the following week. When they report back in the next class, they always describe feeling uplifted. They feel more emotional and empathic, more connected to others. They feel inspired to continue acting altruistically in their daily lives.

So I would like you to do the same: make a conscious attempt to be altruistic. Perform as many acts of kindness as you can. This could mean simply complimenting a work colleague, friend, or stranger — after all, compliments are a form of altruism. Every time you catch yourself thinking a positive thought about someone — that they're doing their job well or that they've made a good meal or cup of coffee — verbalize it.

As you go about your day, put yourself on "altruism alert," looking out for ways in which you can be of service. Offer some food to unhoused people, chatting with them as you do so. Offer an elderly person your seat on the subway. If someone looks lost, offer them directions. If you sense that any of your friends or relatives need support, give them your time and attention.

In a more general sense, consider how wide the circle of your concern stretches and the extent of your service. If you feel that you're mainly serving yourself, make a conscious effort to expand your service to your community or to the world. Devote more of your time, energy, and money to wider causes and concerns.

Let me emphasize that conscious altruism is a spiritual practice, like meditation. Altruism is all about connection: it arises from connection and creates connection. So the more altruism we practice, the more connected we become. And the more connected we become, the more natural altruism becomes to us.

FORGIVENESS AS ALTRUISM

It's easy to be altruistic toward friends and relatives, even to strangers, but what about people who have harmed or wronged us? Do such people even *deserve* our kindness?

In this context, altruism means forgiveness. You might feel that to forgive someone who has wronged you is to condone their behavior or to let them off the hook, allowing them to avoid censure or punishment. However, it's important to remember that forgiveness means being altruistic to *ourselves.*

A few years ago, I met a woman called Sena, whose brother

had been killed while working as a chef in the British army, shot by a soldier from his own unit. His wife was pregnant with their first child, which made his death even more tragic.

Sena's life was thrown into disarray. She had a breakdown, couldn't work or sleep, and was prescribed powerful psychiatric drugs. She didn't leave her house for months. Her condition was made worse by the media attention that the incident created, which lasted for more than two years, through an investigation and trial.

Sena's difficulties continued for several years, until she decided to forgive the man who killed her brother. As she told me, "I realized that it wasn't serving any purpose for me to be so full of hatred and bitterness. All it was doing was causing intense pain inside me.... So I decided to let go. I realized that he was no different to me. He said it was an accident, and I was sure he felt remorse. I knew that it was the right thing to do, to forgive him. And it had an immediate effect. I felt lighter and freer, as if I'd suddenly let go of about forty years of aging. It felt like my life could begin again."

Since then, Sena's life has turned around. She feels that she is a deeper, stronger person living a more meaningful life.

Without forgiveness, we punish *ourselves* by holding on to hatred and resentment. As Sena's story shows, carrying resentment or a grudge against someone drains our energy. It creates inner tension and a heavy sense of negativity that pervades the whole of our lives. In this way, our own resentment allows the person who wronged us to continue hurting us. Forgiveness means releasing resentment so that we ourselves can heal.

So let me guide you through a simple contemplative exercise, a four-stage process in releasing resentment toward a person who has wronged you.

• CONTEMPLATIVE EXERCISE •

Releasing Resentment

Bring to mind a person whom you feel resentment toward because they wronged you in some way. Recall the incident when they mistreated you.

First, let's examine the context of the incident. Try to view the situation from the other person's perspective. Did they actually mean to hurt you? Perhaps it was an accident. Or perhaps their actions were impulsive, carried out without premeditation or intention to harm you.

Even if the person did intend to harm you and has shown no regret, contemplate the factors that may have caused their behavior. Perhaps there are psychological factors, such as low self-esteem, insecurity, addiction, or a personality disorder. Perhaps there are environmental factors, such as a turbulent home life or a difficult upbringing that emotionally scarred them. Remember that people who hurt and humiliate others are usually deeply unhappy themselves.

The second stage is to write a letter of forgiveness to the person. You don't have to mail it (but feel free to do so if you feel inclined). Describe the incident and the hurt you initially felt. Inform the person that hatred and resentment serve no purpose and you have decided to let go of yours. Tell them that you understand why they acted as they did, because of their personality or background. Write that you forgive them and that they — and the incident itself — will no longer preoccupy your mind. End the letter by wishing them well.

Now close your eyes and imagine yourself in a small room, empty except for a table and two chairs. The person who wronged you sits opposite you at the table. You'll probably feel uncomfortable, anxious, with an urge to stand up and leave the room. But don't. Stay where you are, looking at the person opposite you, without speaking. Hold their gaze, recalling the reasons for their ill treatment of you.

Then smile at them. Not necessarily a smile of friendship, but a smile of well-being, showing that you no longer feel resentment toward them, that you are free of negativity. Nod to the person, to show your understanding and forgiveness. Then allow the image to fade from your mind.

Finally, breathe slowly and deeply for a few moments. As you exhale gradually, release any resentment left inside you. Feel the darkness of resentment evaporating. Feel yourself become lighter inside as the heaviness of hatred ebbs away. Take a few more slow and deep breaths, savoring the feeling of freedom. Feel your whole being opening up again, no longer clenched tight by resentment.

BEYOND REVENGE

As a type of altruism, forgiveness shows how the qualities of wakefulness inform and influence one another. For example, forgiveness encourages presence. Resentment is always past oriented, so transcending it means letting go of the past and becoming more present centered. Resentment is also one of the ways in which the thought mind strengthens itself, encouraging rumination and daydreaming. So forgiveness also aids the process of disidentifying with the thought mind.

The opposite of forgiveness is revenge. Revenge might provide a short-lived sense of satisfaction, but it never leads to lasting happiness. In fact, just the opposite: whereas forgiveness brings release, people who take revenge remain attached to the issue and continue ruminating about it, which prolongs their bitterness. In other words, revenge binds us even more closely to the thought mind. And, of course, revenge is never conclusive. It often provokes retaliation, initiating a cycle of violence that leads to more hatred and hurt on both sides.

This is why forgiveness is necessary not just for us as individuals but for the human race collectively. We have a collective responsibility to forgive in order to heal hostility and conflict among different groups and nations. The world is full of conflicts fueled by memories of historical wrongs or ancient animosities passed down from one generation to the next. Unless empathy and understanding prevail, such conflicts intensify over time, bringing more death and destruction. As Archbishop Desmond Tutu, one of the greatest spiritual activists of modern times, wrote, "Forgiveness is an absolute necessity for continued human existence."

BEYOND GROUP IDENTITY

Now I would like to turn to another collective aspect of altruism: transcending group identity, so that we can spread empathy unconditionally to all human beings (and all living beings), irrespective of differences of nationality, ethnicity, or religion.

My home city of Manchester, England, contains the largest cemetery in the UK. A few years ago, while cycling through the cemetery, I realized something that had never struck me before: there were several distinct sections for different faiths — sections for Muslims, Jews, Catholics, members of the Church of England, and so on.

There is nothing unusual about this, of course, but it struck me as absurd and sad. No one is born as a Muslim or Hindu or Christian. All human beings are born as one and the same, without any conceptual labels to differentiate them. The labels are attached to us during late childhood and adolescence, through indoctrination by our parents and our wider culture. By the time we reach adulthood, we associate our identity with the labels and think of ourselves as essentially different from others. As I cycled through the cemetery, it seemed tragic that even in death people were defined by conceptual labels and separated into distinct groups. Surely in death — as in birth — people should be allowed to relinquish labels and return to a state of common identity?

Group identity is responsible for much of the conflict and brutality that has filled human history. Most wars have been fought between two or more opposing groups — religious groups like Catholics and Protestants or Muslims and Hindus; ethnic groups like Serbs, Bosnians, and Croatians, or the Tutsi and Hutu in Rwanda; or ideological factions such as communists and fascists, or the Union and the Confederacy in the American Civil War. Group identity has also led to campaigns of persecution and mass murder, such as the Holocaust or the persecution of the untouchables under the Indian caste system. On a more subtle level, group identity leads to racism and inequality. Human beings are denied justice and opportunity because they are not regarded as individuals, only as members of a different and inferior group.

When we strongly identify with a group, we are liable to restrict our empathy and altruism to our fellows, withholding them from members of other groups. This is what psychologists call "moral exclusion." People from different religions, ethnic groups, or nationalities are excluded from our moral community, and this strong sense of otherness may engender feelings of hostility toward members of different groups. We may perceive them as rivals, feel threatened by them, and blame them for our problems. As a result, it becomes possible for us to exploit, oppress, and even kill them.

This is another way that awakened people differ markedly from others: they don't identify with groups. A need for group identity is the result of ego separateness, creating a sense of lack and insecurity. We crave belonging to groups to assuage our sense of isolation. We crave identity labels to strengthen our fragile egos. But since awakened individuals don't experience separateness, they have no need for identity and belonging. They don't feel affiliated to any particular religion, nationality, or ideology. Nor do they identify themselves as American or Jewish or socialist. They might agree with these terms as a *description*, but they don't derive their identity from these labels or feel any attachment to them.

In the same way, awakened people don't assign group identity to others. They don't perceive people in terms of their religion, nationality, or ethnic group. They see through identity labels to the unique core of every individual. As a result, they treat all human beings with equal respect, regardless of superficial differences. If awakened people have any sense of identity at all, it is solely as global citizens, inhabitants of the planet Earth, beyond nationalities or borders.

In *The Leap*, I described the awakening of a man called Ed, which occurred after a long period of spiritual practice combined with professional failure. Ed lives in the American Midwest but refers to himself only as "a citizen of the cosmos. I don't have any sense of regional or political identity — and around where I live, a lot of people do." I also interviewed two men who described how their attitude to soccer had changed since their awakenings. They both used to be massive fans of their local clubs. Now they had lost the need to support specific teams, although they still sometimes enjoyed watching soccer. As one of the men told me, "Now I just watch football matches and I just think, 'I hope they all win.' I enjoy the game for its own sake."

Now let me guide you through two exercises to help you transcend any notion of group identity. I will take you beyond the illusion of group identity — both in yourself and others — to the common identity of all human beings. We will move past ethnicity, nationality, and religion to the formless essence that expresses itself purely and equally in everyone. In the process, we will become able to extend empathy and altruism to the whole human race.

We will do this both in physical and in spiritual terms, since all human beings are one in both these senses.

• CONTEMPLATIVE EXERCISE •

Beyond Group Identity

In chapter 3, we discussed the intense sense of gratitude felt by astronauts as they gazed at the Earth from space. Another realization that struck many astronauts was that, seen from space, the Earth has no countries or nationalities. There is just one planet, and just one human race. As Rusty Schweickart put it, "You look down there and you can't imagine how many borders and boundaries you cross, again and again and again, and you don't even see them.... You wish you could take a person in each hand, one from each side in the various conflicts, and say, 'Look. Look at it from this perspective. Look at that. What's important?'"

So let's return to the moon. Imagine you're standing on its rocky gray surface, gazing at the Earth 240,000 miles away. You can see the dark blue water that covers most of our planet's surface and the large landmasses between the oceans. You recognize the Earth's continents. You're aware that there are eight billion humans scattered over those continents, together with millions of other species. You see nothing but land and ocean, without borders. There are no nationalities, just groups of human beings inhabiting different parts of the Earth's landmass. The idea of a "nation" is just an abstraction — even an illusion.

Now imagine that history is rewinding back through the centuries. Picture the Earth before the modern era, back through the Middle Ages and the Dark Ages, before ancient Greece and Rome, before ancient Egypt and Sumer, back to when all our ancestors lived a simple hunter-gatherer way of life for millennium after millennium...

Let's rewind history all the way back to 250,000 BCE, when our species developed in what is now eastern Africa. Then let's retrace our steps forward from this beginning. The first Homo sapiens *remain in Africa for tens of thousands of years, but eventually they move further afield, into the Middle East and Europe. (The most significant wave of migration occurs at about 60,000 BCE.) Over the following millennia, as they become more dispersed, different groups develop different physical characteristics in response to new environments and climates. Groups who migrate north develop lighter skin and hair — the further north they go, the lighter they become.*

Differences of language and culture also proliferate. Linguists have identified fundamental vocabulary and grammatical structures shared by all human languages, suggesting that they all stem from one original language, dating back fifty thousand years or more. But as the human race disperses, linguistic variations increase, until groups become unintelligible to one another. At the same time, groups develop their own lifestyles and traditions. They forget their common origin and view themselves as distinct from other groups.

Now let's return to the present day. Consider that every human being you encounter — no matter their skin color, religion, or language — is your relative. If an ancestry website existed that could trace our lineage back to the very beginning, we would find that we all have the same great-great (followed by many other "greats") grandparents.

Whenever you meet a person who seems to belong to a nationality or religion different from your own, remind yourself that identity groups are meaningless labels, randomly imposed by an accident of birth. In essence, no one is a Christian or a Muslim or a Jew, and no one belongs to any nationality. Despite superficial differences, all human beings are your kin — not strangers or enemies, but your cousins. Connect with the essence of every person, beneath the shell of their identity.

• *Meditation: Beyond Individual Identity* •

The above exercise demonstrates that all human beings share the same origin, in physical terms. In the following meditation, we will see that this is true in spiritual terms too.

Close your eyes and settle into your inner being, allowing your breathing and your thoughts to slow down. You may be aware of some thought activity on the surface of your mind. But focus your attention beneath that. Sense the stillness and harmony of your deep being. Return to the space beyond thought and concepts, the radiant emptiness that stretches deep inside you.

There you can feel the dynamic energy of consciousness before it expresses itself in thought. You can sense that energy gently vibrating and flowing through your being — not only through your mental space, but all through your body. This is the essence of your being, your inner spirit.

Let's consider for a moment: Where does this inner spirit — or pure consciousness — come from? Is it produced by your brain and your body? Or does it stem from another source?

With your eyes still closed, bring your awareness outside your body. You can sense a spiritual energy outside you, a subtle dynamic force that fills the space around you. Beyond your room, this spiritual energy fills the air, the sky, and every object on the surface of the Earth. It stretches everywhere, beyond the Earth's atmosphere, through outer space — a dynamic spiritual energy that is the source of all things.

This universal spiritual energy is the source of your inner spirit. It flows into you, through the cells of your brain and whole body, like water into a fountain, creating and sustaining your being.

Let's experience that now. Picture your brain as a kind of radio, with all its billions of cells picking up universal spiritual energy and directing it inside you, so it becomes your own individual consciousness. Feel the spiritual energy flowing through your brain, into your inner being, forming your inner consciousness.

And all over your body, your billions of cells are receiving universal spiritual energy and transmitting it inside you, where it becomes your inner vitality, or energy body. Feel the energy flowing into you, all over your body, replenishing your inner being.

You can sense the oneness of your own inner spirit with the spirit of the universe. You can sense your inner spirit as an influx of universal spirit, like a channel flowing out from a great river. Rest in that awareness for a moment, sensing oneness.

Consider that in the same way that universal spirit flows into you, it enters into every living being on this planet. It becomes the inner spirit of every life-form. It therefore makes you one with every other living being. We are all channels of the same source, with the same spiritual energy flowing through us.

Let's experience that now. Contemplate the people in your vicinity right now, in your building or on the streets outside. They are all manifestations of the same spiritual energy as you. The same spirit flows into them. Feel your oneness with them.

Extend this to other people who are further away, in different cities, countries, and continents, spread over the surface of the Earth. We are all channels of the same source, sharing the same spiritual energy, just as different streams share the same water.

Our oneness enables us to empathize with each other. We can sense each other's pain and joy because we share the same being. Beneath our superficial differences, we share the same essence. We are each other.

As we bring this meditation to a close, let's retain that sense of oneness with universal spirit and with all other living beings. When we encounter other human beings, let's meet them in oneness. Let's recognize our common source, both physically and spiritually, beyond the illusion of group identity.

FELLOW TRAVELERS

A few years ago, I had a spiritual experience at a train station. Arriving early for my train, I sat down for a coffee at the station café, looking around at the other customers and travelers. I was suddenly filled with a tremendous feeling of love for everyone. I felt a strong urge to connect with people, to express my affection through friendliness. Noticing that the man at the next table was wearing a Liverpool football shirt, I started a conversation with him about football. On the train, I chatted with the conductor and joked with the refreshments seller. Looking out the window, I observed sunlight pouring down on the hills under a perfect blue sky, and I felt illuminated too, and as if I was sharing my light with everyone else.

Arriving in the town, I stopped off at a pub for some food. A group of middle-aged men were drinking beer and shouting and swearing. Businessmen talked loudly into their cellphones about customers and deals, while a group of elderly people were complaining about the state of the country. I felt compassion toward them all, as if they were members of my family. I could see the world from all their different perspectives. I sensed our common human identity, our common need for happiness and meaning and purpose, our common need for attention and affirmation to bolster our self-esteem. We were all doing our best to overcome suffering and find wholeness and happiness. I felt exhilarated to be part of the human family in its different manifestations.

It's not uncommon for spiritual experiences to occur in train stations or on train journeys. In my research, I have collected several examples. A man described an experience of sitting in a waiting room at a train station with about twenty other people. Suddenly, for no apparent reason, "I experienced in that moment a sense of profoundest kinship with each and every person there. I loved them all — but with a kind of love I had never felt before.... We were one with each other and with the Life which we all lived in common." Similarly, another man recalled how his train compartment suddenly flooded with light: "A most curious but overwhelming sense possessed me and filled me with ecstasy.... I loved everybody in that compartment. I would have died for any one of the people in that compartment."

Perhaps such experiences occur because stations and journeys remind us that we *are* all fellow travelers. On the one hand, we are all sharing the journey of life, albeit at different stages. At the same time, we are all passengers on the planet Earth as it floats through space, spinning on its axis and rotating around the sun. We all set off from the same place and are heading to the same destination, though we will reach it at different times.

As travelers, we are all equal. We share the same basic impulses, even if we express them in different ways — the impulses to avoid or transcend suffering, to be accepted and respected, to find well-being and love. As we travel together, it makes sense for us to support one another — to help and hold one another, to carry others when they feel weak, to lift others when they fall. It makes sense for us to *connect* with one another, rather than to compete and fight.

A few months after my experience at the train station, I was at a weekend conference where I practiced radical friendliness. I made connection with innumerable conference delegates, as well as taxi drivers, hotel receptionists, and other passengers on buses and trains. As I traveled home from the conference, I had the sense that I had created a large network of connection that would remain in place. In doing so, I felt that I had helped bring a little more harmony into the world and into my own being.

On arriving home, I wrote a poem about the experience.

Making the Human Race Whole

Make as many connections as you can
so that this broken world can become whole again.

It's your responsibility
to radiate benevolence to everyone you meet
to be reckless with your friendliness
and to surprise strangers with your openness
on behalf of the whole human race.

It's your responsibility
to turn suspicion to trust, hostility to sympathy
to expose the absurdity of prejudice
to return hatred with implacable goodwill

until your enemies have no choice but to love you
on behalf of the whole human race.

It's your responsibility
to free yourself from bitterness
and to harness the healing power of forgiveness
to repair connections and reestablish bonds
that were broken by resentment years ago
on behalf of the whole human race.

It's your responsibility
to open up channels of empathy
through which compassion can flow
until there are so many connections
across so many different networks
that, finally, like the cells of a body
billions of human beings will fuse together
sensing their common source
and their common core.

Then a new identity will emerge, an overriding oneness.
And the human race will be whole, at last.

6

ACCEPTANCE

Becoming One with Reality

Awakened individuals live in a mode of acceptance. They don't fight reality with their thoughts. They don't waste their energy mentally complaining about situations that are beyond their control or feeling bitter about past events that can't be changed. If they are ill or injured, they don't get frustrated but relax and rest to allow their bodies to heal. If they have to wait for a long time for an appointment or for service at a store, they don't get agitated, but remain patient and present.

Likewise, awakened people accept fundamental aspects of life that others resist or deny. They accept the aging process, flowing with the slow transformation of their physical form as they move through the process of life. They are happy to think and talk about death, accepting that one day their physical form will naturally dissolve away. Even when tragic events occur — such as bereavement or the diagnosis of a serious illness — they face them with acceptance, rather than shying away from their painful reality. Through acceptance, awakened people are at one with the reality of their lives.

This doesn't mean that awakened individuals are passive in situations of suffering and discord. It doesn't mean that they resign themselves to their own or other people's suffering without trying to alleviate it. As we saw in the last chapter, awakened people *do* usually feel a passionate desire to help others and to contribute to the healing of the world.

In this chapter, we're going to examine and experience the spiritual power of acceptance.

PRACTICING ACCEPTANCE

One morning in August 2000, I was sitting in my flat in Singapore, meditating and enjoying a state of inner calm. Suddenly, for no apparent reason, a loud, high-pitched ringing noise started up in my ear, as if someone had pressed a button. Like everyone, I'd had ringing in my ears for short periods before, so at first I wasn't so concerned. But this ringing didn't go away. In fact, after a few days, it got louder and developed an awful screeching overtone. I found it impossible to meditate and difficult to sleep. It was so loud that I was always conscious of it, unless there was even louder background noise.

I gradually realized that the noise wasn't going to leave me. I had tinnitus, probably due to playing loud music in rock bands when I was younger. The worst thing was that I could never escape the noise — it was always with me, twenty-four hours a day. I used to love silence, to just sit or lie down and listen to stillness, so it was depressing to think that silence was gone forever. I went to see a specialist, who found that I was partially deaf in my ear due to the tinnitus and told me there was no chance of a cure. It was something I'd just have to get used to.

I tried to mask the noise. The specialist gave me a white-noise-generating device to insert in my ear during the day, and at night I went to sleep with the radio tuned between stations. But that wasn't fair to my wife; the noise of the radio made it difficult for her to sleep. Eventually I said to myself, "This is ridiculous. The noise isn't going to go away, so I'll have to try to accept it."

One night I decided not to switch the radio on, but to face up to the noise. Rather than resisting it, I moved toward it; I sank into it and allowed myself to be immersed. And to my surprise, the noise wasn't so disturbing. Imagine there's a person you think of as an enemy and are afraid to meet, but once you face them, you find that they're not so unpleasant after all. I quickly adjusted to the noise and managed to get to sleep quite easily. The next night was even easier. I was less affected by the noise during the day as well and found I could meditate without background noise. Soon all the anxiety and agitation caused by my tinnitus faded away.

I can still hear the tinnitus now — it's ringing in my ear as I write this. But it doesn't affect me. It's just *there*, in a neutral, nonbothering way. I have accepted it as a part of my reality. I no longer resist it, so it doesn't disturb me.

Once I became aware of the power of acceptance through my tinnitus experience, I applied it in other areas of my life. I used it when I was ill with the flu and feeling miserable. I realized that part of my misery was caused by my resistance to the situation. I became aware of my negative thoughts, such as *I haven't got time to be ill! I have deadlines to meet! I'll have to take time off work, and my colleagues will resent me!*

I decided to let go of my resistance. I asked myself, *What's really wrong with this situation? I'm lying down, resting, and as long as I allow myself to rest, I'll get better soon. The deadlines can wait.* I turned my attention away from my thoughts and gave my full awareness to my reality. I looked around the room at the objects surrounding me and the scene outside my window. I paid attention to the feelings inside my body, including my tiredness and discomfort. And immediately, my resistance faded, together with my feelings of negativity. Even my physical symptoms seemed milder.

I followed the same practice one afternoon while stuck in a traffic jam. I had been to the park with my young son, and we were in a long line of cars waiting at traffic lights. After we had been waiting for a few minutes, I became aware of my frustration and impatience, and I suddenly thought, *This is absurd. There's no reason to feel frustrated.* Again, I asked myself, *What's wrong with this situation?* I brought my full awareness to my reality. I became aware of my hands holding the steering wheel, my body on the driver's seat, and my feet pressing the pedals. I was listening to music. I could see a beautiful blue sky, trees by the side of the road. My wonderful son was sitting in the back seat, oblivious to any traffic problems. Again, discomfort faded from my mind, and I felt a sense of ease and well-being.

RESISTING REALITY

It's a normal human impulse to resist adversity. When we suffer, physically or emotionally, we strive to change our situation so that we can return to a state of well-being. When we are hungry, we strive to find food. When we are injured, we take action to aid our recovery. When we are trapped, we try to escape. If we're being bullied or harassed, we try to protect ourselves.

All of this is natural, but we carry this attitude of resistance into many other areas of our lives where it isn't necessary or helpful. We resist everyday situations like illness, traffic jams, or waiting for a bus or train, where our resistance manifests as frustration and impatience. We feel resistance toward our partners and children when they don't behave as we desire. As in my example above, we often verbalize our resistance in thoughts or comments such as *I haven't got time for this! Why does this always happen to me?* or *Will this ever end?* or *Why does he always behave like this?* It may seem natural to feel unhappy in these situations. However, the main source of our unhappiness is not the situations themselves, but our resistance to them.

There is nothing inherently wrong with sitting in a waiting room, until your thought mind tells you that you're being inconvenienced or disrespected. When the anthropologist Edward T. Hall spent time with Native Americans, he was struck that they rarely seemed to be disturbed by waiting. At trading posts and hospitals, Indians never showed any sign of irritation, even if they had to wait for hours. As Hall wrote, "We whites squirmed, got up, sat down, went outside and looked toward the fields where our friends were working, yawned and stretched our legs.... The Indians simply sat there, occasionally passing a word to one another." In other words, the Indians had an attitude of acceptance to the situation, while the European Americans had one of resistance.

The Buddha beautifully illustrated the harmful effects of resistance with his teaching of the two arrows. The first arrow, he said, is the suffering that we inevitably experience as human beings, including physical illness and pain. The second, much more dangerous arrow is our *resistance* to our suffering, including negative thoughts, judgments, and hostility toward others. When negative events occur, we worry about the future, complain about other people who have caused the events, chastise ourselves for our mistakes, and feel envious of those who have avoided misfortune. According to the Buddha, the second arrow of mental suffering is completely unnecessary. Simply by accepting our predicament, we can free ourselves from mental pain.

Without the second arrow, the suffering of the first arrow

becomes more tolerable. In fact, it may even disappear altogether. For example, research has shown that the best way of dealing with physical pain or discomfort is not to try to avoid or mask it but to be *mindful* of it. When we accept and bring our attention to pain, it becomes softer and milder. (I'll share an exercise to illustrate this later.)

Acceptance can encourage the healing process too. Think of an athlete who is injured and can't practice or compete for several weeks. With an attitude of resistance, they feel frustrated and impatient. They don't rest or relax properly and may decide to start playing again before they're ready, causing more damage. But with an attitude of acceptance, an athlete recovers more rapidly, partly because they allow themselves to rest more deeply, but also because acceptance creates harmony between the mind and body.

We're encouraged to think of illness and pain as enemies. We speak of "beating" an illness or "fighting to get better." But mentally, this attitude isn't helpful. Resistance to illness or physical discomfort simply intensifies and prolongs our unhappiness. In resistance, the mind is in conflict with the body, resenting it for its weakness and pressuring it into getting better. But in acceptance, the mind fully supports the body, becoming one with it and allowing powerful healing energies to flow.

THE THOUGHT MIND AS ARCHER

Resistance stems from the thought mind. In the Buddha's analogy, the thought mind is the archer who shoots the second arrow. It has its own vision of how our lives should be, which is always different from how our lives actually are. Our thoughts create expectations that reality usually doesn't live up to. They create visions of alternate realities that are supposedly superior to our present reality. They tempt us with desires and ambitions for future happiness that make us feel dissatisfied with the present. Rather than accepting what is or what has been, the thought mind speaks in terms of "could haves" and "should haves" or "could have beens" and "should have beens."

Resistance inevitably leads to discord. It creates conflict between us and reality, since our thoughts are opposed to what is. It creates duality, since there is a gulf between our desires and reality. Resistance also drains our energy. It takes a lot of energy to resist reality, to constantly make a mental effort to oppose our experiences and predicaments, like soldiers trying to protect a fort that is under continual attack.

As a result, to live in resistance means to live in discontent. Correspondingly, acceptance means to live in contentment, in harmony and oneness with reality.

• CONTEMPLATIVE EXERCISE •
Varieties of Resistance

The first stage of cultivating acceptance involves becoming aware of the areas of our lives where we practice resistance. Here I will discuss six typical areas of resistance, allowing you to contemplate whether any apply to you.

Resistance to the past. *Do you find aspects of your past difficult to accept? Are there experiences that feel painful when you contemplate them, such as wrong decisions or missed opportunities? Perhaps every so often your mind returns to these situations, and you find yourself imagining alternative scenarios, daydreaming about how different your life would be if you hadn't made those mistakes.*

We can't change the past, so resistance to it is futile. It creates a completely unnecessary second arrow of frustration and regret. The only choice we have is to change our attitude to the past, from resistance to acceptance.

Everyday resistance. *How do you respond when you encounter inconvenient everyday situations, such as long lines, traffic jams, or awkward dealings with companies or colleagues? Do you immediately become impatient and frustrated, maybe even lose your temper?*

Perhaps you also feel some resistance to certain tasks or chores that are part of your daily life — such as household chores that you consider boring or aspects of your job that make you feel uncomfortable. Or you might feel resistance toward certain people you encounter regularly, because of their personality or behavior or their past treatment of you.

Resistance to illness or injury. *How do you respond when you are ill or injured? Do you habitually add the second arrow of mental suffering to your physical symptoms?*

Resistance to your life situation. *Are there aspects of your life situation that you feel resistance toward, such as your job, marriage, or living environment? Perhaps you feel that your job doesn't suit or fulfill you, and spend a large part of your day wishing you were doing something else. You may have a similar attitude to your house or town. Or perhaps you feel dissatisfied with your partner, wishing you were with someone who was more loving, more responsible, or better looking.*

Of course, there's nothing wrong with wishing to change your life situation. It may be entirely healthy and right for you to alter your career path or end your relationship. But that doesn't mean you have to spend your days in resistance, opposing the reality of your life. While preparing for and initiating change, you can still accept your life situation as it presently is. In fact, this will make you more capable of making necessary changes, with the clarity and energy that acceptance brings.

Resistance to traumatic life events. *From time to time, we all go through traumatic events in our lives, such as serious illness or injury, relationship breakdown, or bereavement. How do you respond to these events? Do you refuse to acknowledge them, distracting yourself from their painful reality? Or do you have the courage to face up to them?*

Of course, it's very difficult to meet such major challenges with acceptance. However, this certainly is possible (as we will see shortly). In fact, acceptance of such experiences may have a powerful transformational effect, leading to spiritual awakening.

Resistance to life itself. *Do you resist fundamental aspects of life itself, such as the aging process and death? Do you resist the slow transformation of your physical form that occurs with age and try to maintain an illusion of youth? Do you avoid thinking about death and feel uncomfortable when others mention it?*

As with some of the strategies we use to escape the present (discussed in chapter 4), resistance to aging and death is partly due to cultural conditioning. Western secular cultures worship youth, denigrate old age, and treat death as a taboo subject. So it's not surprising that many of us struggle to accept these fundamental realities.

THE ALCHEMY OF ACCEPTANCE

Before we turn to some exercises to cultivate acceptance, let me illustrate the powerful, wide-ranging effects of acceptance by sharing a poem with you.

The Alchemy of Acceptance, Part 1

Emptiness can be a vacuum
cold and hostile, dark with danger
or emptiness can be radiant space
glowing with soft stillness
and the only difference between them is acceptance.

A task may seem tedious
a chore to rush through reluctantly
or a task may seem rewarding
a process to relish with an attentive mind
that reveals more richness the more present you become
and the only difference between them is acceptance.

Pain may seem unbearable
searing through you from a sharp, concentrated point
so that you have no choice but to resist
to try to escape, to push away the pain
or pain can be a sensation
that you move toward and merge with
that no longer has a center and dissipates through your being
until it becomes soft and numb, no longer pain at all
and the only difference between them is acceptance.

Trauma can break you down to nothing
destroy the identity you spent your whole life building up
like an earthquake that leaves you in ruins
or trauma can transform you
break open new depths and heights of you
give rise to a greater structure, a miraculous new self
and the only difference between them is acceptance.

Life can be frustrating and full of obstacles
with desires for a different life constantly disturbing your mind
or life can be fulfilling, full of opportunities
with a constant flow of gratitude for the gifts you have
and the only difference between them is acceptance.

• *Meditation: Accepting Physical Pain* •

I've mentioned how important it is to meet pain and discomfort with acceptance, and the next meditation will help you to do this. You can apply it to your own pain (now, or the next time you experience any pain) or use it to help a person close to you, in which case you can read the text to them out loud. The third verse of the poem above (beginning "Pain may seem unbearable") is based on this meditation.

This practice is very familiar to me because I often guide my wife through it, when she has migraines. As any migraine sufferer knows, the pain can be so severe that you can't do anything but lie down in darkness, waiting for it to pass.

When you experience physical pain or discomfort, you may feel an impulse to escape from the pain, to move away from it or try to suppress it. But don't do this. Instead of resisting the pain, move toward it. Locate the source of the pain, its epicenter, and bring your attention to it.

As you move toward the pain, allow your attention to merge with it. The pain isn't your enemy — it's just a signal telling you that a part of your body or being needs some care and attention. So don't be afraid of the pain. Embrace it. Become one with it.

As you merge with the pain, it loses its sharpness. It grows softer. Rather than being concentrated into a single sharp point, it begins to dissipate. It spreads through your being like ice melting into water. As it spreads, it seems to dilute, becoming even softer.

Now it no longer feels like pain — it's just a soft, numb sensation, throbbing gently. You are one with the sensation. It's part of you. You can feel it pervading your whole being. But now it feels so soft that it doesn't disturb you. It feels almost pleasant, this soft, numb sensation, gently pulsating through your inner space.

• CONTEMPLATIVE EXERCISE •
Releasing Resistance

Now let me guide you through a more general exercise on acceptance, based on the six areas of resistance I highlighted above. We're going to identify any areas of your life where you experience resistance and then transform that resistance into acceptance.

Let's contemplate different aspects of your life. As we go through the following areas, be mindful of any places where you feel resistance. We will return to these later in the exercise.

First, consider your past. Are there any negative events that you keep returning to in your mind — opportunities that passed you by, random misfortunes that derailed your progress, or mistakes that you made?

Now let's consider your body. Are there are any physical ailments or injuries that cause you discomfort on a regular or ongoing basis? Perhaps you can even sense them right at this moment.

Let's consider the tasks and activities that constitute your daily life — your household chores, your family responsibilities, the duties that are part of your job, and so on. Perhaps there are some responsibilities (or even people) that create resistance.

Let's consider your life situation. Do you feel any resistance to your job or profession, your living environment, or your close relationships?

Now consider traumatic life events, such as a relationship breakdown, serious illness, bereavement, or perhaps a friend or relative who is facing a serious challenge. You may not be dealing with any of these issues right now, but you've no doubt had to deal with them in the past, just as you will in the future. Do you meet such events with acceptance or try to push them out of your awareness?

Finally, let's turn to life itself. Do you feel resistance toward the aging process? Do you feel resistance toward the prospect of dying, so much so that you try to avoid thinking about death?

Let's return to one of the areas where you noted some resistance. Bring the activity or situation into your mind. As you contemplate it, be mindful of the negative feelings and thoughts you associate with it. Be aware of the space between you and those feelings and thoughts. Remind yourself that you are the observer of the contents of your mind, watching from a distance, as if sitting on a riverbank watching the river flow by. Remind yourself that you don't have to let those thoughts or feelings determine your mood. You can remain untouched, in a state of well-being and calmness.

Now imagine a cord that connects you to this situation or activity. It is attached very tightly, creating tension.

We will now release your resistance, in coordination with your breathing. Take a long, deep in-breath. Then, as you breathe out deeply and slowly, imagine that the cord that connects you to the situation is dissolving, melting away. As it does so, feel your resistance fading. Feel the tension evaporating. Feel yourself opening more widely, embracing the reality of your life. If you like, as you exhale, say aloud, "I release my resistance."

Repeat this process until you feel that your resistance to the situation has completely melted away.

Then choose another area of your life that creates resistance and repeat the process. However, you don't have to deal with every area straightaway — feel free to address other areas during another session, on another day.

To finish, let me guide you through a visualization exercise. Picture yourself sitting or standing on the side of a high mountain or, if you like, at the peak of the mountain. Beneath you and all around you, you see a landscape — the landscape of your life. You can see your past, stretching from your birth to the present. You can see all the tasks and activities and people that are part of your current daily life — your household chores, the tasks of your job, your family responsibilities, the people you regularly encounter, and so on. The landscape also includes your life situation — your profession, your relationships, your living environment, and the like. You can also see fundamental aspects of life, such as the aging process and death.

Survey the landscape and accept it all, exactly as it is. Imagine stretching your arms out wide, opening up your chest, and embracing every aspect of your life. Open yourself completely to the reality of your life. Accept and embrace the whole of your reality as it is, right now.

As you do this, you feel a sense of liberation and lightness, now that you've laid down the burden of your resistance. You feel a sense of inner harmony, now that you're no longer fighting against reality. You feel a sense of oneness, now that your mind is aligned with what is.

This doesn't mean that your life is in an ideal state. It doesn't mean you don't need to change anything. In fact, as you open yourself to the landscape of your life, you can clearly sense some areas of imbalance or discord, where change is necessary. And moreover, with your new clarity and energy, you now have the power to make the changes.

THE MIRACLE OF ACCEPTANCE

Now you can sense the alchemy of acceptance — the wonderful shift that occurs when we replace resistance with acceptance. Conflict and tension melt away, replaced with ease. Duality fades away, as we become one with the reality of our lives. We experience a sense of release and relief, now that we're no longer making a constant effort to oppose reality. The energy we utilized to resist reality is freed, making us feel stronger and more alive.

Perhaps most strikingly, situations that we found uncomfortable and even intolerable no longer disturb us. When we're in a mode of acceptance, some situations become simply neutral, while others actually become enjoyable. Tasks that seemed tedious become pleasurable. Situations that seemed mundane and unsatisfying become fascinating and fulfilling. Rather than mentally complaining about situations in a state of abstraction, we return to awareness, and our experiences become fresh and rich. In these moments, we realize the truth of the Stoic philosopher Epictetus's statement that people "are disturbed not by things, but by the views which they take of things." We realize that the situations seem unpleasant only because of our negative attitude toward them.

Of course, some situations inherently involve suffering, such as pain, illness, abuse, or oppression. But even here an attitude of acceptance has a healing effect. Pain becomes softer; suffering becomes milder. Discord seems less disturbing. An attitude of acceptance also brings greater stability and resilience, making us aware that we have the resources to endure and overcome the situation. This even applies to traumatic major events like serious illness or injury, divorce, or bereavement. Once we acknowledge and accept them, they become more benign. Even while facing our own death, acceptance can create equanimity and harmony.

In fact, in traumatic situations, a mode of acceptance may give rise to sudden spiritual awakening. In my book *Extraordinary Awakenings*, I described the phenomenon of "transformation through turmoil," when intense psychological suffering breaks down a person's ego, allowing a latent spiritually awakened self to emerge, which then becomes their new identity. In my research, I found that this shift often occurs when the person is in a mode of acceptance. Some people could identity a specific moment when they let go or gave up their resistance to their predicament. In some cases, they felt they had no choice but to accept their state, as they had nothing left to cling to or to hope for. For instance, a man called Kevin experienced a sudden shift when, as an alcoholic engaged in the AA recovery process, he "handed over" his problem in a mode of surrender. Another man, Michael, became disabled after a fall while he was running. He underwent transformation when he heard a voice inside his head say, "Let go, man, let go. Look at how you're holding on. What do you think life's telling you?"

This is the most radical way in which the alchemy of acceptance manifests itself. But hopefully you'll undergo a similar — though gradual and less dramatic — shift while practicing the exercises in this chapter.

ACCEPTANCE IS NOT RESIGNATION

As transformation through turmoil shows, acceptance is not something that we actively do. It is a release of effort, rather than an effort in itself. It is something that we *stop doing* — namely, resisting reality. In acceptance, we drop our weapons and surrender to reality. And rather than feeling defeated, we become more empowered.

This links to another important point about acceptance, one that I've touched on already but would like to emphasize. Acceptance doesn't mean passively accepting oppression, abuse, or trauma. It doesn't mean not asking for help or not reporting or confronting people who harm us. Acceptance is not the same as *resignation*. To accept that you have cancer doesn't mean avoiding or refusing treatment. In fact, accepting and embracing your diagnosis — rather than treating it as an enemy to fight against — may improve your chances of recovery by creating equanimity, with a harmony between body and mind that may encourage the healing process. Similarly, to accept that you are addicted to drugs or alcohol is the first stage of recovery.

Acceptance is often the starting point for necessary change. With acceptance, we gain the resilience, energy, and clarity to create transformation. We gain a clear sense of which aspects of our lives, if any, are out of balance and causing discord, and therefore need to be changed. Within the harmony of acceptance, a strong and pure impulse arises to improve our situation and alleviate our suffering. This is how we enhance our lives, in accordance with our deepest needs.

EMBRACING REALITY

Is it really possible to accept every aspect of my life? you might wonder. However, remember that all qualities of wakefulness naturally grow stronger as we cultivate them. As our lives become more harmonious through acceptance, that harmony begins to exert its own influence, bringing further balance and alignment. As with gratitude, an attitude of acceptance will pervade every aspect of our lives and become our normal mode of meeting every experience, like hosts who greet every guest with hospitality.

Acceptance is not weakness, but courage. It is the courage to live without delusion or self-deception, to face reality no matter how painful or mundane it may appear. And thanks to the alchemy of acceptance, once we embrace reality, it ceases to feel painful or mundane. We become aware that the source of suffering is not reality itself but our resistance to reality. Acceptance brings us into oneness with reality. And in oneness, there can never be suffering.

The Alchemy of Acceptance, Part 2

Old age may be a process of decay
that withers your body and mind
and poisons you with bitterness
as you yearn for the freshness of youth.

Or old age may be a process of liberation
that enriches you with wisdom
and makes you more present as the future recedes
and lightens your soul as you let go of attachments.

And the only difference between them is acceptance.

Death may be a cold, black emptiness
that mercilessly devours your ego

and makes everything you own seem valueless
and everything you've achieved seem meaningless.

Or death may be a perfect culmination
a soft twilight at the end of a long summer's day
when you're filled with heavy tiredness and ready to sleep
and know that you will wake up again to a bright new dawn.

And the only difference between them is acceptance.

7

INTEGRATION

Harmony with the Body

Spiritual development carries a risk of imbalance. For example, if we live as monks or recluses, we run a risk of neglecting the relational and practical aspects of life. As I mentioned earlier, this may mean that any wakefulness we develop is fragile and lopsided, easily disrupted by the stresses and demands of everyday life. To become deep-rooted and stable, awakening has to incorporate every aspect of our being and our lives.

Spiritual development carries a particular risk of imbalance in relation to the body. Some spiritual teachers and traditions neglect the body, even viewing it as an enemy or obstacle. However, in this chapter, I will show you that the body is integral to awakening. As we undergo awakening, we do not leave the body behind or transcend it — we carry it with us.

We've seen that awakening means an expansion of awareness and an increasing sense of connection, and this applies to the body too. Just as awakening intensifies our perceptual awareness, it intensifies our awareness of and experience of the body. Just as awakening brings an enhanced sense of connection to nature and other living beings, it brings an enhanced connection to the body.

In this chapter, we will explore and cultivate this enhanced relationship to the body. We will also find that a harmonious relationship with the body can encourage the overall process of awakening, helping us to cultivate other qualities.

AMBIVALENCE AND HOSTILITY

Although oneness, or nonduality, is an essential principle of spirituality, some traditions have a (somewhat contradictory) dualistic attitude to the body. They see the spirit and the body as two different entities, which live together uneasily, like two roommates who have nothing in common. The spirit is seen as pure, the source of our highest qualities, while the body is corrupt, the source of our basest instincts. The body drags us down to the level of animal, while the spirit lifts us above the material world, into a realm of truth and harmony. Not surprisingly, this perspective creates an ambivalent, if not downright hostile, attitude to the body.

This type of attitude is common in monotheistic religions, which view spiritual development as a battle between the spirit and the flesh. This was the basis of the appalling practices of some Christian ascetics, who punished their bodies by wearing hair shirts, iron chains, and belts of nails. Such traditions saw sexual instincts as base and animalistic, part of the lower body that we must transcend. This led to sexual repression and guilt, a belief that the natural and healthy impulse for sex was sinful. Before Christianity, the ancient Persian religion of Zoroastrianism believed that the whole material world, including the human body, was corrupt and evil, and only the soul was "good." In a similar way, the tradition of Gnosticism viewed the body as a prison containing a tiny hidden divine spark that would be released at death.

Some traditions don't directly denigrate the material world

and the body but view them as illusions. This is the view taken by some extreme forms of Advaita Vedanta, which hold that only brahman (or spirit) is real and that the whole material world is a dream in the mind of brahman. In a similar way, some modern-day nonduality teachers tell us that only consciousness or awareness is real and all the events and experiences that appear in our consciousness are just projections, like the images on a cinema screen. Since it consists of matter, the body is part of the illusion. This doesn't necessarily mean we should mistreat the body or repress our instincts. But it does devalue the body, suggesting it is of little importance, in the same way that a dream has less importance than reality.

THE AWAKENED BODY

As I see it, this attitude to the body (and to the world in general) represents a kind of partial, imbalanced spirituality. A holistic form of wakefulness perceives no duality between the spirit and the body or between the spirit and the world. The healthiest, most integrated form of wakefulness views the body and the world, not as separate from but as *imbued with* spirit. The body is not opposed to spirit; it is a physical expression of spirit. We should therefore cultivate harmony between the material and spiritual aspects of our being.

Many spiritual traditions do take this view. Varieties of Buddhism such as the Ch'an, Zen, and Tibetan traditions emphasize the sacred and spiritual nature of all reality, including the human body. The Tantric traditions of Hinduism and Buddhism insist that all parts of the body, as well as all physical processes, are infused with spirit. In the West, Tantra is sometimes seen as being all about sex, but sex is just one aspect of the body that is sacred and that can be used as a spiritual practice. One Tantric text, the Jnanarnava Tantra, even goes so far as to proclaim that "faeces, urine, menstruation, nails and bones" are sacred and pure. In a similar way, in his poem "I Sing the Body Electric," the great awakened poet Walt Whitman lists dozens of different parts of the body, then states, "O I say these are not the parts and poems of the Body only, but of the soul, / O I say now these are the soul!"

AWAKENED ATTITUDES TO THE BODY

In my research, most awakened individuals share the positive attitude to the body expressed by Whitman and the above traditions.

In the normal human state, many of us feel a sense of separation from our bodies, in the same way that we feel separate from other people and from the world itself. Rather than seeing the body as an integrated part of our being, we perceive ourselves as mental entities who live inside our bodies, like passengers driving a car. This — along with a lack of appreciation due to the taking for granted syndrome — means that we may neglect and even abuse our bodies, just as we are liable to disrespect people whom we perceive as "other" to us.

But in awakening, we transcend this dualistic view of the body, along with all other dualities. We realize that we *are* our bodies — that they are not an enemy or an obstruction, but part of our spiritual nature. We sense no duality between the material and the spiritual: like the whole world itself, the body is pervaded with spirit. In other words, awakened individuals experience a sense of oneness with the body, rather than separateness. Mind and body become an integrated whole, like old friends who live together harmoniously in a house.

After awakening, many people report that they feel more

present in their bodies and more aware of them. The physicality of their bodies becomes more real in the same way that their surroundings become more vivid. This was described to me by Parker, who had a sudden awakening after a period of suicidal depression. He told me how he suddenly became "aware of all the different parts of my body. It was as if my soul had been occupying this body for my entire life but I never gave a second thought to what it felt like until now, or I just wasn't paying attention to the feeling of living in my body."

This heightened awareness of the body brings increased physical sensitivity. Many awakened people report that food seems to have more flavor and that physical activities (such as swimming, running, or sex) become more intense and pleasurable. In a similar way, they experience increased sensitivity to the needs of the body. After awakening, many people change their diets, usually by eating more organic food and becoming vegetarian or vegan. As a woman named Cheryl told me, "I became a vegetarian.... I try to eat organic food and as much raw food as I can. I don't want to put unnatural things in my body or in my house. It's as if through being more connected to things, I've become more aware of the difference between natural and unnatural."

In the same way that they value and respect other people more, awakened people treat their bodies with more care and attention. They are reluctant to harm their bodies through habits such as smoking or drinking alcohol. They may feel the impulse to avoid (or at least reduce their intake of) substances like sugar or caffeine. They often start doing more physical exercise, particularly psychospiritual practices such as yoga or qigong. Again, all these changes stem from a new, positive relationship to the body.

A NOTE OF CAUTION: TRAUMA AND THE BODY

Before I guide you through some body-centered exercises, a note of caution: If you've undergone a significant amount of trauma that hasn't yet been processed or healed, you may have a difficult relationship with your body. Trauma is often held within the body, creating a sense of recoil or even hostility toward our physical selves.

However, I would still encourage you to try the exercises, provided you're in a calm and stable frame of mind. As I hope I conveyed in the last chapter, the best approach to pain (both physical and mental) is not to avoid or repress it but to move toward it, with an attitude of acknowledgment and acceptance. At the same time, I recommend that you proceed carefully, with a therapist or close friend at hand to create a sense of safety and to provide support if needed. And of course, if the following exercises do begin to cause significant discomfort, you should stop immediately.

ONENESS WITH THE BODY

Let me guide you through a meditation that will help you to sense the sacred, spiritual nature of your body and bring you into oneness with it. The meditation is divided into two parts, focusing on two different aspects of the body. First, we'll focus on the physical body, then on the inner energy of the body. I will demonstrate that both these aspects of the body are spiritual in nature.

To introduce the meditation, here is a poem.

Your Body Is Not a Burden

Your body is not a beast
whose instincts debase you
whose functions demean you
and whose desires corrupt your purity.

Your body is not a burden
whose ailments disturb you
whose impulses irritate you
and whose demands must be satisfied
before your soul can express itself.

Your body is not a prison
that will confine and constrict you until you die
when you'll finally be released from suffering
and fly into the ether, like a bird out of its cage.

Relax and let your sense of self expand
beyond the boundaries of your mind
through your chest and arms and your waist and legs
through your bones and veins and muscles and organs
until every molecule of your being
is alive with your energy and attention.

Then you'll sense the sacredness of your body
how every supple movement of your limbs
every fine-honed form of your tissue and bones
and every process that flows inside you
from your breath to your pulse to your blood
is as spiritual as your soul.

• *Body Meditation 1: Oneness with the Physical Body* •

First, let's focus on the physical body, following a similar process to the one in the poem above.

Think of your self-awareness as a spotlight. Most of the time, the spotlight of self-awareness is confined to our minds. We identify solely with the mind and view the body as merely an appendage or a vehicle.

But now let's widen the range of the spotlight. Let's expand our self-awareness throughout the body.

Bring your attention to the solid reality of your body. Sense the physicality of your head — your skull, the hair growing from your head, the sockets of your eyes, your cheekbones, and your jaw and teeth. Be aware of the skin and tissue of your face, of your eyes and nose.

Move your attention lower, to your shoulders. Feel their sturdiness and solidity, how they support your head and frame your upper body. Bring your attention to your upper arms, then down toward your elbows and forearms. Feel the strength and flexibility of your arms, with their bones, muscles, and tendons. Then bring your attention down to your hands and fingers, feeling their dexterity, how they clench and stretch and bend.

As your awareness expands in this way, your sense of self expands to encompass every aspect of your body. Your body is not an appendage. It is not a material object that you inhabit. It is part of you. It is you.

Bring your attention the center of your body, to your chest and upper back, then your stomach and lower back. Feel the strength and solidity of your torso, your ribs protecting your inner organs, and your spine holding you upright. Again, be aware of the skin and tissue that cover those bones.

As you sense the different parts of your body, be aware that their physical solidity is pervaded with spirit. All things in the world are pervaded with spirit — all natural forms, all human-made objects, and all space. All material things are manifestations of spirit, and all contain spirit. This applies to every part of your body too. As you bring your attention to different parts of your body, be aware of their spiritual essence. Feel spiritual energy vibrating inside them.

Now bring your awareness to your lower body — the soft flesh of your bottom and the sturdy bones of your thighs, down to your knees. Feel the thinness of your shins, the points of your ankles, the curvature of the soles of your feet. Feel all your toes.

Now sense your body as a whole, all parts at the same time. Feel the fullness of your physical body as your being. Feel how your entire body is alive with awareness and imbued with spirit. Sense spirit pervading every atom of your body, just as sunlight shines over all objects on the surface of the Earth.

• Body Meditation 2: Oneness with the Energy Body •

Now switch your attention away from your physicality to the inner energy of your body. This is the vitality, or subtle energy, that flows through your physical body. Some esoteric traditions refer to it as the subtle body. You may have heard it referred to as chi in Taoism or prana in Hinduism. Every physical aspect of your body has an energetic equivalent, like a mirror image. In chapter 5, I suggested that this inner energy is an influx of universal spiritual energy, received and transmitted through the cells of the body.

The best place to start this process is the palms of your hands, where we often feel this subtle energy tingling. Bring your attention to both palms, taking care not to focus on their physicality, but on the energy you can feel inside them. Once you sense that tingling energy, feel it flowing inside your fingers too, and the rest of your hands. Feel it flowing inside your arms, up to your shoulders, then up to your head. Feel how, in your head, it merges with the dynamic inner energy of your consciousness.

Feel this dynamic energy flowing inside your chest and stomach, down to your waist, then down into your legs, your knees, and your feet. Now you can sense that each physical part of your body has an inner energetic aspect, in the same way that your brain has an inner aspect of mind or consciousness.

Now feel the entire energy field of your body flowing through the whole of your physical body. Be aware that this energy field includes your consciousness. There is no distinction between your mind and your body. They are one, alive inwardly with the same spiritual energy.

Now be aware of the two spiritual aspects of your body at the same time. Sense the sacredness of the body in both its physical and subtle forms. Sense the spiritual nature of the body, how every part is shining with spirit, both outwardly and inwardly, both physically and energetically.

• LIFE PRACTICE •

Presence through the Body

In chapter 2, I described how the body can help us to disidentify from the thought mind. By bringing awareness to physical and biological processes, we also become aware of thinking as a process. We realize that we don't have to identify with our thoughts, just as we don't have to identity with our heart beating or with our digestion.

In a similar way, the body can be a powerful aid to presence. This is because the body is always solidly, firmly, physically in the present. Wherever your mind might be — ruminating over past events, creating scenarios of future events, or daydreaming about alternate realities — your body is always here in the world. It is rooted in the present like an anchor. It can never be anywhere but here. While your mind restlessly jumps to different points of time, mulling over what happened last night or could happen tomorrow, your limbs are moving through the present, your heart is beating along with the present, your lungs are breathing the air of the present.

Learn to use the body as a gateway into presence. Whenever you recognize that you are absent — in a state of abstraction or absorption — you can use the simple strategy of transferring your attention from your mind to your body. Give yourself a gentle mental nudge (the phrase I used in chapter 4) into awareness of your body.

Here's a simple example: When you're struggling to get to sleep at night, perhaps because your mind is too busy, bring your attention outside your mental space, into the solid reality of your body. Be aware of your breathing, the sensations of the air brushing your nose, and your stomach rising and falling with your breath. Feel the firmness of your whole body on the bed. Mentally scan your attention slowly through your body, from your head down to your shoulders, your chest, all the way to your feet. While your attention is focused inside your body, your thoughts will soon slow down, and you'll drift off to sleep in a state of relaxed presence.

The same applies to your waking moments. If you're walking down the street in a state of abstraction, paying more attention to your chattering thoughts than to your surroundings, simply bring your attention into your body. Feel the sensation of walking, your limbs moving through the air and your feet pressing against the ground. Without the fuel of attention, your mind will slow down, like a car that runs out of gas. Then, as you shift from abstraction into awareness, your surroundings will become more vivid, and your experiences will become more real.

Your Body Is Always Here

The thought mind never comes to rest.
It's always shifting from the future to the past
like a wild, swirling river
whose currents keep changing direction.

But beneath your restless thought mind
lies your body, firm and fixed
like the hard floor of a riverbed.

While the mind flits from daydream to daydream
the body is always here.
When the mind is clouded with abstractions
the body is always real.

So when streams of thought are flowing wildly
anchor yourself in your body.

Give your attention to your limbs and muscles
rather than to your mind.
Locate yourself in your skin and bones
instead of the future and past.
Listen to your heartbeat and your breath
instead of your chattering thoughts.
Feel the weight of your body beneath you
and the space it occupies in the world.

And soon your turbulent mind will lose momentum
slow down and come to rest
like water settling after a storm.
The boundaries of your mind will soften
and the energy of your inner body
will flow into your mental space
like fresh air through an open door.

Then your mind and body will rest together
grounded firmly in the world.

PRESENCE THROUGH EXERCISE

As a young man, I lived a very unhealthy life. I smoked about thirty cigarettes daily, drank endless cups of coffee during the day, then switched to beer in the evenings. My diet was poor, and I never consciously did any exercise. (I didn't drive, though, which meant that at least I got some exercise by walking and cycling.) I thought of my body as a machine whose condition or appearance didn't matter very much, so long as it functioned. I spent almost all my time indoors, writing or reading at my desk or playing or recording music, and usually stayed up till the early hours of the morning, waking up around lunchtime. As described in *The Leap*, I had always had a degree of natural wakefulness, but it was overlaid with confusion and self-dislike, with the feeling that I would never feel at home or be able to function in the everyday world.

However, at the age of twenty-nine, I started to meditate regularly for the first time in my life and met the woman who is now my wife. I built up self-esteem and confidence and found that I could deal with everyday life and ordinary social relationships after all. As a result of these changes, my wakefulness began to stabilize.

During this period, my attitude to my body shifted. I gave up smoking and drinking beer (not coffee, although I cut down a lot!). For the first time, I started to think about diet; I made a conscious effort to eat more healthily and became a vegetarian. I took up yoga and swimming and started to go for long walks in the countryside.

Since then, exercise has become a bigger and bigger feature of my life. I started running at the age of forty, joined a local gym at forty-five, and then began to play tennis, badminton, and squash, as well as regularly playing football in the park with my kids and their friends and parents.

The reason I love exercise isn't so much because of its physical benefits but because of its mental and spiritual effects. Exercise generates presence. This is particularly the case with solitary types of exercise, such as running and swimming. I love running in the early morning, feeling the breeze against my body, gazing at the trees and the sky and the sun. The rhythm of running works like the repetition of a mantra in meditation, slowing and settling my mind. At the end of a run, I feel alert and energized. I feel at one with my body, as if my awareness has spread to every cell.

My favorite type of exercise is swimming outdoors, in lakes or the sea. I love the feeling of the water massaging my limbs as I swim. Again, the repetitive motion seems to have a meditative effect, making me more mindful and alert. I feel at one with the water, enjoying a deep sense of belonging, as if I've returned to an ancient home.

In my view, this is the main reason why so many people love physical exercise, even if they're not consciously aware of it: because it brings presence. It shifts us out of abstraction or absorption into awareness. It releases us from confinement in the thought mind. When a period of exercise is over, our thoughts flow more quietly and slowly, and our minds and bodies seem to merge. Physical activity heals the duality between mind and body.

In this sense, exercise is active meditation. Over the years, I've met many people who love the idea of meditation but find it difficult to practice. When they sit down and close their eyes, they find that their minds become more restless, and their attention naturally gravitates to worries and fears, which seem to intensify. When such people ask me for advice, I usually suggest they practice *active* meditation instead. I point out that many activities have a meditative effect without being meditation per se. I advise them to start running or swimming, going to the gym, or walking in nature. These activities will bring some of the benefits of meditation, quieting their minds and expanding their awareness. Once they've practiced this for a few months and their minds have become more settled, they may be able to sit down and practice meditation in its traditional sense.

• LIFE PRACTICE •
Active Meditation

Ensure that you regularly practice some form of exercise, such as running, swimming, walking in nature, or competitive sports. As I described above, exercise is a simple but effective technique for generating presence. It's a great way of increasing the amount of time we spend in awareness, rather than in abstraction or absorption. It also helps to connect our minds with our bodies, reminding us that they are two complementary aspects of spirit, not enemies that can't coexist.

In addition, active meditation through exercise is a way of treating our bodies with the respect they deserve. When we consider the millions of miracles that take place inside our bodies every moment of the day, the precious and fragile processes that maintain our health and our life, then it's natural to treat the body with care and respect. And, of course, exercise also helps to maintain these processes.

GRATITUDE TO THE BODY

Unfortunately, many people take their bodies for granted. They forget the fragility and intricacy of the myriad processes that sustain their lives, all finely tuned to keep them healthy and conscious. Combined with the sense that the body is "other" to them, taking-for-granted-ness makes them prone to neglect and even abuse their bodies by eating unhealthily, using drugs and other harmful substances, and not exercising.

However, once awakening frees us from the taking for granted syndrome and brings a new awareness of and integration to the body, the opposite occurs. We recognize the body as miraculous, and our health as precious. Following her close brush with death during a terrorist attack, Gill Hicks described how she was "in awe of my body; I was in awe of the human spirit.... I made a promise, a vow, that I would look after myself, love myself every day. I would feed my body good food."

We briefly expressed our gratitude to the body in chapter 3, as a part of a general exercise on gratitude. But here is a fuller expression of gratitude to the body. I recommend doing this meditation at least once a week, as a reminder to treat your physical being with the reverence it deserves.

• *Meditation: Gratitude to the Body* •

Let's rekindle a warm inner glow of gratitude. If you like, again recall (as we did in chapter 3) a past situation when someone was kind or generous to you and you were filled with intense gratitude. Allow that gratitude to fill you again now, radiating from your heart, expanding and intensifying.

Now spread that glow of gratitude through your body. Begin with your vital organs. Direct the warm glow of gratitude to your lungs, your stomach, your kidneys, and your heart. Thank them for the work they are doing right now to keep you healthy and alive and conscious. Thank them for the support they have given you every moment of your life.

Now, moving outward, extend the warm glow of gratitude to your bones, spreading it through your whole skeleton. Thank them for their solidity and strength, for their support and protection throughout your life.

Next, moving further outward, extend the glow of gratitude to the limbs and muscles that cover your bones. Thank them for their flexibility and power, for allowing you to move freely through the world.

Extend the glow of gratitude to your veins and arteries, which carry blood around your body. Thank the skin that covers your bones and muscles, encloses and holds your body, protects you from injury, and regulates your temperature.

Also be mindful that your body contains millions of microcosmic processes, far too small for you to see or sense, which are helping to keep you alive and healthy. Processes of cleansing and healing and digesting, of absorbing nutrients, of metabolizing energy, of fending off viruses and bacteria. Extend the warm glow of gratitude to these microcosmic processes, aware that your life depends on all of them.

Now feel that sense of gratitude glowing through your body as a whole. There are so many intricate, interconnecting processes taking place inside you, keeping you alive and conscious from moment to moment, that your existence is a miracle. So be grateful for the miracle of your existence, created and sustained by the service of your body.

As we finish, consider again the spiritual nature of your body. Sense spirit pervading every atom of your physical body, just as it pervades every atom of the world, flowing through your bones, muscles, veins, and inner organs. Then return your awareness to your subtle body, the energetic equivalent of your physical body. Sense the spiritual nature of that inner energy, how your own life energy is a channel of the spiritual energy of the universe.

There is no duality between the flesh and spirit. Your body is one with spirit. Your body is spirit.

8

DETACHMENT

Freedom from Psychological Attachments

What is the main source of happiness in your life? Do you try to find happiness by buying and owning material goods or accumulating wealth or status? Do you derive happiness from substances like food or alcohol or from electronic devices that provide you with entertainment? Is your happiness a future project of hopes and ambitions or a byproduct of your job, which makes you feel productive and useful? Or does your happiness stem from religious or political beliefs that bring cohesion to your life, providing purpose and meaning?

For most of us, happiness is conditional. It derives from and depends on external sources. Although there's certainly nothing wrong with enjoying entertainments and pleasures or having ambitions or beliefs, if your happiness stems solely from external sources, it is always fragile and unstable. It can easily be disturbed when external conditions change. External sources of happiness also divert us from the most fulfilling and reliable source of well-being, which is internal: not an unstable condition of the world, but a natural condition of being.

External sources of happiness are closely bound up with identity. As well as providing us with pleasure and satisfaction, our possessions, roles, achievements, and ambitions give us a sense that we are *someone*. We can prove that we exist because we have an identity as a mechanic, teacher, or author, or because we have labeled ourselves a Christian or Muslim or Scientologist or Republican. We can point to our possessions and achievements as further evidence of our significance. On a more ongoing basis, status and success bring respect from others, which also reminds us that we exist.

We're so dependent on all these identifiers that when they're taken away — as they all will be, sooner or later — the effect is often devastating. When we lose our possessions or success or physical beauty, when our hopes and beliefs are revealed as illusions, or when we lose our professional or family roles — these are usually crushing, traumatic blows that lead to depression or breakdown. Without these external conditions, our happiness evaporates, and our identity crumbles. We feel depressed, empty, and exposed, no longer sure of who we are.

Awakened people don't derive their well-being and identity from possessions, success, or ambitions. It's not important for them to be wealthy or admired for their achievements. They aren't particularly concerned about their physical appearance. It may well be that they are physically attractive, that they have attained some degree of success or status, or that they have strong professional or family roles. But their sense of well-being and identity doesn't derive from these things. When events bring changes and these conditions fade away, they don't feel any sense of loss.

This is why awakened people tend to live simple, quiet lives in modest surroundings, eating simple foods and wearing simple clothes, with a minimum of possessions. They don't need external sources of happiness because they have access to an internal source of well-being and identity, which sustains itself through all the many shifting situations and conditions of life.

DETACHMENT

A straightforward way to express this is to say that awakened people live in a state of *detachment*. I don't mean detachment in the sense of indifference or disconnection, but in the sense of being unattached to external sources of happiness or well-being. Detachment is a state of inward contentment and self-sufficiency, without dependence on possessions, achievements, roles, status, and ambitions.

This doesn't mean that awakened people live as ascetics, denying themselves pleasures or comforts or possessions. It doesn't mean that they are Luddites who refuse to use smartphones or the internet. It just means that they're not dependent on these things. As a result, they are moderate in their use of them and don't feel a sense of lack or discomfort when they are taken away.

Awakened people don't mind being successful, but equally they don't feel disappointed when success fades away. They are happy to adopt professional or family roles but aren't disturbed when a job ends or when their children leave home to start college. Since they don't derive their identity from external conditions, they are affected little (if it all) by such changes. As the Bhagavad Gita describes it, the awakened individual is "the same in pleasure and pain, to whom gold or stones or earth are one, and what is pleasing or displeasing leaves him in peace."

All spiritual traditions emphasize the importance of freedom from psychological attachments. For example, both Buddhism and Christianity advise us to live simply and moderately, taking no more than we need from the world. They encourage us to be humble, unattached to notions of achievement and success. They urge us to appreciate our blessings and be content with our present life situation, rather than attached to desires and ambitions. Both traditions also encourage awareness of death as a way of weakening our attachment to possessions, achievements, and other worldly concerns. (We'll look at this in more detail in the next chapter.)

In a more extreme way, adepts across all traditions may follow paths of *renunciation*. Renunciates, who often live as monks, practice voluntary poverty, give up personal ambitions and achievements, relinquish professional roles and family life, and usually practice celibacy. Although, as I've already suggested, this way of life carries the risk of imbalance, it stems from a recognition that attachments are an obstacle to spiritual development and that to live without them brings inner freedom.

Attachments clutter our inner being and obscure our spiritual essence. The more we derive our identity from them, the more alienated we become from our essential harmony and wholeness. And the freer of attachments we become, the more powerfully our inner harmony and wholeness express themselves.

THE PARADOX OF LOSS: SELF-RETURN

You've probably experienced the liberating effect of detachment already at certain points in your life. Perhaps it was a situation when your hopes and ambitions were dashed — when you realized you weren't going to make it as a singer or an actor, that a relationship was over, or that your religious beliefs were illusions. After the initial shock of disillusionment, you may have felt an unexpected sense of relief and liberation. Or perhaps it was a situation where you relinquished a role — when you left a profession after many years, or when your children left home, taking away your role as a parent. After an initial feeling of emptiness and disorientation, perhaps you felt a new authenticity, as if you had uncovered a deeper identity.

In these situations, it's as if the part of ourselves we gave away to external sources is returned to us. As a result, we feel stronger, more stable and whole. I refer to this as *self-return.*

On a simple level, we experience self-return when we let go of possessions. This is why it feels so liberating to off-load material goods: we release our psychological attachment to them. We de-clutter, not just our houses, but also our inner beings.

A dramatic example of this is a man I knew who lost all his possessions. He was moving to a different city to start a new job, and one Saturday morning he packed all his belongings into his van. Before setting off, he decided to have a last cup of tea with the flatmates he was leaving. Fifteen minutes later, the van was gone, stolen while he was drinking tea. At first, he was devastated: he had lost his clothes, furniture, family heirlooms, books, electrical equipment, and the van itself — everything he owned. He spent most of the day in a state of shock. However, by the time he went to bed that night, he felt euphoric, light and free, as if he had let go of a massive burden. The loss made him realize that he had accumulated way too many possessions and that he didn't need them to be happy. From that point on, he lived a simpler way of life.

Self-return also occurs on release from addictions. You may have felt a sense of liberation and self-return after giving up an addiction like smoking, coffee, even sugar or junk food. After a short period — perhaps a few weeks — of discomfort, your inner being starts to heal. A new strength and wholeness grow inside you, as if the part of yourself you gave away to the addiction is returned.

This occurs on a more profound level on release from drug

or alcohol addiction. Drug or alcohol addiction means giving *everything* away, as these addictions take over our whole being, becoming the motivation for everything we do. Recovering addicts sometimes remark that they've "been given my whole life back," but strictly speaking they have been given their *whole selves* back. Every aspect of their being that was subsumed by their addiction is returned to them: their creativity, their capacity for love, kindness, and trust, their gratitude, the ability to enjoy simple pleasures, and more.

It's also common to undergo a natural process of detachment as we grow older, through relinquishing roles and ambitions and letting go of our attachment to appearance. Some people resist the loss of these attachments and become embittered, wishing they were still young and attractive or feeling redundant without their roles. But for many others, aging is a natural process of spiritual development, bringing new freedom and contentment. This is probably why research shows that, across different countries and cultures, the over-sixty-fives are the happiest age group.

This is the paradox of loss: that true contentment comes, not from what we gain, but from what we relinquish; that the initial pain of separation from our attachments turns into the joy of freedom.

Loss

In every loss lies liberation.

When we're adrift in the future
chasing after goals and ambitions
loss pulls us back to the present.
When illusions of success and status

have inflated our self-importance
loss returns us to reality
and reminds us of our insignificance.

When our minds are full of confused desires
loss disentangles us
and simplifies our lives
so that we have space to grow.

When there are too many attachments inside us
obscuring our true nature
loss empties out our being
and reconnects us to our essence.

Loss breaks down our identity
so that our broken fragments
can fuse together again
at a higher level of order.

In loss we find ourselves again.

TRANSFORMATION THROUGH TURMOIL

Detachment is the key to understanding the phenomenon of transformation through turmoil. As I described in chapter 6, this is when intense psychological suffering breaks down the ego, leading to spiritual awakening. Ego breakdown happens in one of two ways. First, it can be triggered by sudden shock or intense psychological pressure, such as a bereavement or a period of intense stress. The ego can't withstand the pressure and collapses, like a house in a hurricane. Second — and more commonly — ego breakdown is due to a loss of psychological attachments. Attachments are the building blocks of the ego, so when enough of them are removed, the ego itself collapses, like a house when enough bricks are taken away. This can happen through a diagnosis of cancer, when the prospect of imminent death breaks down our attachments. It can occur through a long process of addiction, when we gradually lose everything — our friends and families, our careers, our possessions, even our homes. A long period of depression may have a similar effect, leading to a complete loss of hope, even a loss of the will to live.

In these moments, the loss of psychological attachments is usually the reason *why* we are in turmoil. We feel broken because our attachments are broken. The beliefs, hopes, status, possessions, or roles that provided us with a sense of well-being and identity are removed, leaving us bereft and empty. In this sense, the term *breakdown* is perfectly apposite. The breaking of our psychological attachments leads to a breakdown of the ego itself.

However, for some people — a small minority — breakdown also means a shift up. As their ego dissolves, a spiritually awakened self emerges inside them, like a phoenix from the ashes, and establishes itself as their new identity. This spiritual self was always there, dormant beneath the ego, waiting for the opportunity to arise. As noted in chapter 6, this transformation is often initiated by a shift into a mode of acceptance.

This new spiritual self is so different from their old self that many "shifters" (as I refer to people who experience transformation through turmoil) feel like they have become a different person living in the same body. For example, Gill Hicks remarked that she felt that she was living "Life Two," with a new sense of gratitude and purpose. A woman called Glyn, who underwent a shift following the death of her daughter, described her shift as being "like the transformation a caterpillar goes through during the chrysalis stage before emerging as a butterfly." Similarly, Eve underwent a sudden awakening after years of severe alcoholism brought her to a point of complete desolation, culminating in a suicide attempt. As she told me, "My whole psyche changed completely. I have no trauma, in spite of all the terrible things I went through. It was like being catapulted from one world into the next."

These examples — and the phenomenon of transformation through turmoil generally — illustrate the profound spiritual power of releasing psychological attachments and why detachment is an essential quality in awakening.

THE JOURNEY OF ATTACHMENT

Why do we need attachments? Why is it so important for us to reinforce our identity through roles and labels and to accumulate possessions and achievements?

Let's return to childhood. We've already noted some parallels between young children and awakened individuals, such as their presence, heightened awareness, and connection to the world. Another parallel is that young children live in a state of natural detachment. They aren't interested in the future, so aren't attached to ambitions and hopes. Although they love playing with toys, they don't accumulate possessions for their own sake, nor are they attached to their appearance. Although some parents foist religious beliefs on them, children don't normally form a strong attachment to religious beliefs until late childhood or adolescence.

Young children don't need attachments because they have no sense of separateness. They don't experience themselves as individual entities, inhabiting their own mental space. Separateness develops during late childhood and adolescence, as the ego establishes itself as a structure. An inner voice starts to speak, commenting and ruminating, and we begin to live inside ourselves rather than in the world. The world seems to be out there, on the other side.

This is one of the reasons — perhaps the most fundamental one — why adolescence is often a troubled time. After a state of natural connection and presence, adolescents have to adjust to living as separate egos, alone and apart from the world. They feel a painful sense of fragility and vulnerability, as if they're tiny, flimsy fragments that have been broken off from the whole. The sheer *enormity* of the world of otherness out there may feel overwhelming and threatening. They also have to adjust to the restless thought chatter that has started to stream through their minds.

As we enter adulthood, we accumulate attachments to try to compensate for our sense of separateness and alleviate our fragility and vulnerability. In order to strengthen ourselves and build up our identity, we gather possessions, knowledge, beliefs, and ambitions. We collect roles as professionals and parents. We amass achievements, status, and perhaps power and wealth. There is certainly a cultural element to this process too, as with our incessant activity and our resistance to the aging process and death. We are encouraged to accumulate by the materialistic values of our culture, by pressure from parents and peers and advertisements.

If all goes according to plan, by the time we reach middle age we have built up a strong identity based on our attachments. We possess so many building blocks that our ego feels solid and sturdy, like a fortress. We feel confident, stable, and strong, able to function in society. We're no longer flimsy fragments but hard, solid blocks that can withstand the pressures of life.

However, the negative side is that our ego identity — and all the attachments it consists of — separates us from the essence of our being. Our attachments disconnect us from our true selves and from the world itself. In this way, attachments actually worsen the problem they're meant to solve. The stronger our ego grows, the more disconnected we become. The fortress that protects us increases our isolation.

For some people, a growing alienation from their true selves manifests as a midlife crisis. By middle age, they have accumulated so many attachments that they have completely lost contact with their essence. They feel empty and bereft, because they have lost themselves. Their inner being is cluttered with too many attachments, causing pressure, weighing them down, leaving no space for their essence to shine through. The midlife crisis is their inner being crying out for space and light.

Some people respond to this crisis by making fundamental changes to their lives and letting go of their attachments. Some may even come to realize that true well-being doesn't stem from external conditions and so begin to explore their inner being, perhaps through meditation or other spiritual practices and paths. However, many people simply feel depressed and confused. They try to escape their suffering by accumulating even more power and possessions or living more hedonistically.

After the midlife crisis, as they move toward old age, some people may go through the natural process of detachment that I described earlier. Approaching death, they may even completely let go of their attachments and die in a serene state of acceptance. In this way, they come full circle and return to the natural detachment of early childhood.

• CONTEMPLATIVE EXERCISE •

Becoming Aware of Attachments

The first stage of letting go of our attachments is to become aware of them. As I pointed out earlier, awareness is liberating in itself.

Simply becoming aware of an issue helps to free us from it. This is particularly true with attachments, since we are often unaware that we carry them. We pick them up without realizing it. They become so ingrained that we express them habitually, without conscious awareness. Some we carry for so long that we forget about them, like items we absentmindedly place in our pockets.

I'll now list some types of attachments. I would like you to consider whether — and to what degree — you are attached to each of them. You could think in terms of a scale from one to five, one being the smallest degree of dependency and five, the largest.

Don't be disappointed if you find you have a lot of attachments or if you score high on some items. It's unrealistic to expect to be completely free of attachments. Perhaps only the most intensely awakened people live without any psychological attachments whatsoever.

We'll begin with the more overt forms of attachment, before moving to more subtle conceptual forms.

- **Substance addiction.** *Are you physically or psychologically addicted to substances like alcohol, drugs, cigarettes, coffee, or junk food?*
- **Electronic devices.** *Are you psychologically addicted to your smartphone or computer? To your email or social media accounts?*
- **Possessions and money.** *Do you accumulate possessions and money? Do you derive identity from your material goods, such as your car, house, clothes, and electronic gadgets?*
- **Appearance.** *Do you derive identity from your looks, spending a lot of time caring for your appearance, striving to look attractive or to hide signs of aging?*
- **Beliefs.** *Do you derive identity from religious, political,*

or spiritual beliefs, strengthening your ego with ideological labels or through a sense of belonging to a group?

- **Status, success, or power.** *Do you derive identity from the status and success you have accumulated or the power and influence you wield? Do you have a history of achievement — perhaps reinforced through qualifications, awards, and promotions — that makes you feel significant?*
- **Knowledge.** *Do your derive identity from the knowledge and expertise you have collected, perhaps through your profession or your cultural or spiritual pursuits? Do you try to impress other people with this knowledge?*
- **Social roles.** *Is your identity bound up with your professional role or your role as a parent or caretaker or spouse? Ask yourself,* Who am I? *If your immediate answer is* I'm a writer/lawyer/teacher *or* I'm a father/mother, *then you probably do mainly derive your identity from these roles.*
- **Hopes and ambitions.** *Do you derive your identity from a future image of yourself and your life? Does your well-being depend on ambitions, hopes, goals, and the feeling that you are progressing toward them?*

To help determine your level of dependency, consider how you would feel if these attachments were taken away. For example, how would you feel on a trip to a country where alcohol is illegal, where you couldn't have a drink for two weeks or more? How would you feel if you lost your internet connection and had no access to email or social media for a few days? How would you feel if your present success turned to failure or if you lost your professional identity? How comfortable do you feel about the aging process and your changing appearance?

There is nothing wrong with any of the things you might be attached to in themselves, provided they don't endanger your health or other people's well-being. In my view, it's fine to drink coffee and even alcohol in moderation. There's nothing wrong with keeping some beautiful artifacts in your home or other objects that hold meaning. There's nothing wrong with relishing your physical form and taking care of your appearance. There's nothing wrong with acquiring knowledge, having hopes or ambitions, or enjoying a professional role.

Problems arise only when we become psychologically attached to these things and depend on them for our identity and well-being. In fact, without dependency, we can enjoy a healthier relationship with our professional roles, our bodies, food and drink, material objects, other people, and so on. Without the tension of clinging to them or the fear of losing them, we can savor them more fully.

RELEASING ATTACHMENTS

Once we are aware of these attachments, how can we free ourselves from them? I recommend three main exercises, which should be used in combination: a contemplative exercise, a life practice, and a detachment meditation. (There is also a fourth exercise, focused on love and attachment.)

The first exercise is a visualization similar to the releasing resistance exercise we practiced in chapter 6.

• CONTEMPLATIVE EXERCISE •
Releasing Our Attachments

Close your eyes and sink into your inner space. Locate the place beneath the surface of your mind where you can sense the harmony of your deep being. Feel the natural well-being and wholeness at your essence.

Choose one of the attachments that you identified from the list in the previous exercise. Create an image of the attachment or of something that you associate with it. Imagine a cord connecting you to the attachment. Feel the tightness and heaviness of the cord. Sense how the attachment restricts you. It ties you down, stops you moving freely, binds you.

Return to the sense of harmony within you. Tell yourself, I no longer need this attachment. I don't need to derive my identity or happiness from an external source. There is a deep source of well-being and wholeness inside me that doesn't depend on anything external.

Take a long, deep in-breath. Then, while exhaling slowly, tell yourself, I release this attachment. *Imagine that the cord that connects you to the attachment is dissolving and disappearing. As the cord dissolves, you feel a release of tension and a sense of liberation. A feeling of lightness and openness fills you.*

Straightaway, you sense healing. The part of your being that you gave away to the attachment returns to you. You feel more complete, more authentic. You feel stronger, more whole, more stable.

Repeat this process with one or two further out-breaths, reinforcing the sense of freedom and openness.

• LIFE PRACTICE •

Conscious Detachment

The above exercise may be sufficient to release you from some shallow or light attachments. In most cases, however, you'll also need to combine the exercise with an ongoing practice of conscious detachment.

Conscious detachment should already be familiar to you. It's a practice that we routinely follow whenever we want to break or change our habits — for example, when we decide to stop smoking or to give up caffeine or alcohol. It simply means making a conscious effort, by exercising restraint and willpower, not to connect with our attachment.

For example, if you're attached to electronic devices or the internet, follow up the previous exercise by establishing some guidelines for yourself. Limit the number of times you check your email or social media accounts each day. Give yourself long periods — including whole days — where you don't use the internet at all. You'll be surprised at how quickly your attachment fades away and a sense of self-return arises.

Similarly, if you're attached to your appearance, combine the exercise with a conscious attempt to detach yourself by, for example, off-loading some excess clothes, avoiding looking at your reflection, or refraining from dyeing your hair. If you're attached to possessions, make a conscious effort to downshift by off-loading some of your possessions. If you're attached to status, let go of some of your positions or roles.

Conscious detachment allows the habitual reflex of attachments to fade away. Soon inner strength and wholeness will arise. As you experience self-return, you'll realize that you don't actually need *the attachments. Far from being the source of your happiness, they were an obstacle to true well-being. You could compare the situation to that of a teenager who's been raised by overprotective parents and so lacks confidence. But once they leave their parents and move to a different city, they quickly find that they can cope. They discover that they are more capable than they realized and feel a powerful sense of liberation and autonomy. The same process occurs when we release attachments.*

It's important to trust your inner being. Even when we let go of the deepest and heaviest attachments — the ones that we doubt we can live without — an initial period of loss and discomfort is always followed by healing. Our essential self grows into the space left by the attachment. By letting go of external sources of happiness and identity, we gain greater access to the deep essence of our being.

Remember that letting go of attachments is a long-term process, like the adventure of awakening itself. Deal with one attachment at a time, using the two previous exercises, repeating them as needed. You can also practice the longer detachment meditation that I'll describe shortly.

Be realistic too: no one is expecting you to become completely free of all attachments. It's a question of degree. But every degree of detachment you gain is a step toward freedom and true well-being.

LOVE AND ATTACHMENT

One issue that often comes up when I discuss attachment at workshops is love. What's the difference between attachment and love? Is love a form of attachment? Is it wrong to be attached to other people?

It's true that many relationships are based on unhealthy attachment. Dependency makes some people stay with partners who disrespect or abuse them, because they feel that they can't cope on their own. (Coercive people purposely increase their partners' dependency by weakening their sense of independence and confidence.) In some marriages, dependency continues long after love has dissolved away, prolonging the unhappy relationship beyond its natural end.

Dependency can be an issue in other types of relationships too. We sometimes maintain friendships with people we don't particularly like or have little in common with because we're afraid of loneliness or ostracism. Parents sometimes have a dependent relationship with their children. Afraid of letting them go, they don't allow them to develop independence and feel jealous when they find romantic partners. Some of us may become attached to celebrities, obsessively following them online and longing to meet them in person.

However, attachment is not love. In fact, paradoxically, attachment in relationships is based on separation. In attachment, we bind ourselves to another person, as if with cement. No matter how tightly we attach ourselves, a boundary always exists, in the same way that there is always a boundary between two building blocks that are placed together. We always remain essentially apart and alone.

Such relationships are never harmonious, because intimacy and trust can't pass through the solid barrier between us. We can never truly connect with the other person. Such relationships are always insecure, often full of jealousy and conflict, because they aren't rooted in a stable connection. They also feature a fundamental imbalance: dependent partners often feel that they're not receiving enough support, while their partners feel overburdened with the weight of attachment.

However, in love there is no separation and therefore no attachment. Personal boundaries fade, and two people become one. Imbalance and insecurity disappear, since we are no longer separate individuals bearing our own weight, pushing and pressing against each other. Intimacy and trust flow naturally between us. Without dependency, loving relationships are based on support and equality and are infused with harmony.

• CONTEMPLATIVE EXERCISE •

Who Are You Attached To?

Contemplate the people in your life: your partner (if you have one), your relatives and friends. Are your relationships with them based on love or attachment?

If you identify a relationship that is based on attachment, practice the releasing attachment exercise. Visualize a cord that connects you to the person. Exhale slowly, imagining that the cord is dissolving away. Then practice conscious detachment toward the person. Abstain from their company temporarily, until the attachment weakens and self-return arises.

Then, when you resume contact with the person, free from attachment, the relationship will become healthier. Without insecurity and resentment, you'll connect to the essence of their being, beyond the ego, forming a deep bond of trust.

On the other hand, you may find that you don't want to renew relationships with some people. It may feel more congruent to end your relationships with them and free yourself from their malign influence.

Love and Attachment

Since I love you, I'm not attached to you.

If I were attached to you
I'd add myself to you, like baggage.
I'd weigh you down and slow you down
and you'd resent me and try to off-load me.

And the harder you tried to free yourself, the tighter I'd cling
and the heavier I'd become.
Then we would struggle and wrestle like enemies, not lovers.

But we're not two separate entities
bound together as if with glue.

We merge with each other, without boundary.

Our souls have grown deeper and wider
because we share each other's inner space.
We step softly and lightly through life
because we walk as one.

We aren't a burden to each other
because we are each other.

Since I love you, I'm not attached to you —
I am you.

• *Detachment Meditation* •

This meditation (also partly a contemplative exercise) is the third main practice to help you release psychological attachments. I recommend practicing it in conjunction with conscious detachment and the releasing attachments exercise. Lasting around twenty minutes, this extended meditation will reattune you to your innate wholeness and well-being, removing the need for psychological attachments. Any craving to reattach yourself to a substance, object, concept, or person will fade, and you will rest in the harmony of your essential being.

The practice begins with a visualization.

Imagine that you're walking down a long, straight road into the future. The road stretches in front of you as far as you can see. Some future events — arrangements, plans, deadlines — are visible by the side of the road.

The road stretches behind you as well, as far back into the past as you can see. As you look behind you, some events from your past are visible on either side of the road.

Watch yourself walking along this road for a short while, toward the future and away from the past.

Far ahead in the distance, a thick, gray mist emerges and starts to cover the road. It moves toward you slowly like foam, covering the road and the events along its sides.

As the mist draws closer, you can sense its softness and warmth. It brushes gently against your skin, then keeps foaming behind you, covering the road and the events from your past.

Now the mist covers the whole of the road, both ahead of and behind you. You can see nothing but foaming gray mist. There are no directions — no future ahead of you, no past behind. But after a few seconds, the mist begins to disperse. Light gradually breaks through, like dawn breaking through morning fog. As the fog dissipates and the light grows brighter, a natural landscape emerges — a landscape of trees, fields, flowers, and hills, with blue sky above.

The fog has completely gone. A beautiful natural scene stretches around you, clear and bright. You can see plainly now that your life is a panorama, without any forward or backward direction. There is no future or past, only the panorama of the present. You sense clearly that the future and the past are unreal. You can never be anywhere except here, in the present.

So now, consciously release your attachment to the future and the past. Allow your attachment to dissolve, to melt away, feeling space opening around you. If you like, as with the releasing attachment exercise, coordinate this action with your breathing: that is, release your attachment to the future and past as you exhale. As you let go, feel your tension evaporate. Feel a sense of lightness and openness filling you.

Now we'll go through other psychological attachments and let go of them one by one.

Consider any attachment you have to possessions or to money. Remember that there is nothing you can truly own. There are only objects that you can use for a while, then set aside, like tools that you put down after use. Nothing belongs to you except your body and inner being.

With this in mind, release your attachment to possessions or money. As the attachment dissolves, feel a further release of tension. You feel lighter, more open and spacious inside.

Let's contemplate your attachment to beliefs or belief systems — perhaps religious beliefs, political beliefs, or more general beliefs about people, life, or the world. Consider that beliefs are simply old thoughts that have become rigid and ingrained. Your beliefs belong to the past. They stop you from perceiving situations objectively and responding to events spontaneously.

So now, release your attachment to your beliefs. Again, feel a release of tension as you let go, a sense of lightness and openness.

Let's turn to your attachment to knowledge — the knowledge you have accumulated in certain areas, which may bring a sense of pride and superiority. Consider that knowledge is simply memory. It also belongs to the past. It can be useful, but it doesn't define you. Here in the present, the only knowledge is the direct knowledge of experience.

So now, release your attachment to your knowledge. Again, coordinate this with your breathing if you like. As you let go, feel a release of tension, with an increasing lightness and openness.

Now let's turn to your attachment to achievements, success, or status. Perhaps these create a self-image of you as a significant and special person. Consider that all your achievements belong to the past. Like knowledge, they are nothing more than memory. None of them exist now, in the present. In a similar way, your status or success is simply a concept, an idea in your mind (and other people's), based on your past achievements.

So now, release your attachment to your achievements, status, and success. As you let go, feel the tension releasing, replaced by a sense of lightness and openness.

Now contemplate your attachment to your appearance. Consider that life is a process and that your body naturally changes as a part of this process. Resistance to the process only causes conflict and tension. Also consider that the essence of your being has no physical form and no actual appearance. When you interact with people, it is this essence that they respond to, not your appearance.

So now, release your attachment to your appearance, feeling an increasing lightness and openness.

Let's consider the concept of age. Remember that the essence of your being has no age, just as it has no physical form. The essence of your being is timeless, eternal. So now, release your attachment to the concept of age. As you let go, you feel even lighter, even more spacious and open.

Finally, let's consider your name. Consider that your name is just a sound, given to you by your parents for ease of communication. The essence of your being has no name, just as it has no physical form or age. Your name doesn't define you, any more than your roles or possessions do. So release your attachment to your name, with a sense of further lightness and openness.

You've now released your attachment to the future and past, to possessions, beliefs, knowledge, achievements and status, appearance, your age and name.

What remains at the end of this process?

What remains is the pure essence of your being, pure consciousness without form. This essence has natural qualities of wholeness and well-being. You can feel those qualities inside you right now.

As you experience these qualities, you sense clearly that there is no need for attachment. There is no need to seek happiness or identity from external sources. There is an innate well-being and wholeness at the core of your being, shining like the sun, always accessible to you.

For a few moments, rest within the essence of your being, in a state of pure detachment and pure well-being.

Now bring your awareness back to the sounds inside your room. Feel the points of contact where your body meets the floor and your chair.

Open your eyes and bring this meditation to a close.

THE ESSENCE

The radiant spiritual essence I've just described has been a recurring theme of this book as we've moved through the different qualities of wakefulness. It's the translucent inner light that is uncovered as the clutter of attachments and the chatter of thoughts dissipate, as our beings grow clear and calm, like the sun that appears as clouds dissolve. Just as the sun is the source of light, this essence is the source of spiritual well-being, of the deep harmony beneath the turbulent surface of our minds.

The essence isn't just our true self, though: we share it with all other human beings and all living beings. It's the place where our individual being meets and merges with universal spirit, the source of our own consciousness and that of every other being, allowing us to sense our oneness with all. That's why we feel at peace and at home here: because we have reached the source of being.

The Essence

The essence of you is emptiness
the essence of you is love
the essence of you is energy
the essence of you is bliss.

The essence of you flows like a fountain
from a pool of pure consciousness at the heart of reality.
The essence of you surges with an eternal force
that has borrowed you for this lifetime.

The essence of you is deathless.
This form will wither and dissolve away
then the essence will return to its source
to find a new expression.

The essence of you stretches
inside and outside your body
inside and outside time
within and beyond the world
at home, in peace, in love.

9

EMBRACING MORTALITY

Awakening through Awareness of Death

When I was younger, I spent a lot of time thinking about death. At the age of sixteen, it suddenly struck me that I was a mortal being, that I was inevitably going to die at some point and in fact could die at any moment. All it would take was an accident, or for some part of my body to randomly malfunction, and my life would come to an abrupt end. It also struck me that I had power over my own existence — that if I wanted to, I could end my life at any moment by suicide. It was a revelation. I had always taken my life for granted, but now I realized it was temporary and fragile.

This awareness didn't depress me, though. On the contrary, it provided a sense of freedom and perspective. It made me aware that life is precious and shouldn't be wasted. It was too valuable for me to spend my days watching television or working at a mundane, unfulfilling job. It was too important for me to let opportunities pass by or to procrastinate. It was too brief and fragile for me to worry about trivial things like possessions and status or other people's opinions of me. It was too precious to carry around resentment or feel bitter about past events.

In my twenties, my main interest was music. I played in various bands, usually as bass guitarist and singer, and wrote a lot of songs. Once our drummer asked, "Steve, why are so many of your songs about death?" It had never occurred to me before, but I realized he was right. We were playing songs with titles like "It's Only Life," "Mourn the Death of Mankind," and "I Hope I Don't Die Tonight." I think this is one of the reasons why, despite our best efforts, none of my bands attained any real success: our songs were too doom laden to have mass appeal.

I'm not so different now. (I no longer write songs, but I do write poetry!) I still often contemplate my mortality, sensing that life is fragile and precious, and this awareness still provides a sense of freedom and perspective. Perhaps the only real difference is that I no longer assume that death is the end. Back then, I thought there was nothing on the other side of death, just extinction. (As I wrote in one of my songs, "Eternal nothingness is just an accident away.") Now I feel strongly that death isn't oblivion — that when my existence in this body and in this world comes to a close, there will be some form of continuation. I sense something inside me — a spiritual essence — that will outlast my physical form. Nevertheless, I still feel that my life in this form and in this world is a blessing, a precious gift that I should appreciate and make good use of.

• CONTEMPLATIVE EXERCISE •

What Is Your Attitude toward Death?

In chapter 4 on presence, I mentioned the three A's of abstraction, absorption, and awareness. Now I want to introduce another set of three A's. These denote three different attitudes we typically take toward death: avoidance, anxiety, and acceptance. As I describe these, contemplate which one applies to you.

Avoidance. *Do you view death as a taboo subject? Do you shy away from thinking or speaking about it, assuming it will make you feel uncomfortable? When you must address the topic, do you use euphemisms like "when something happens" rather than speaking about it directly? Do you dismiss any discussion of death as "morbid" or "unhealthy"?*

Death avoidance is certainly encouraged by our culture. If sex was the great taboo of Western cultures in the nineteenth century, death is the great taboo of the modern age. Earlier cultures had a much more open attitude to death, and people made conscious efforts to remind themselves of their mortality. In Victorian times, people wore mourning veils for years after a bereavement, together with lockets containing the hair of their deceased loved ones. Some modern-day cultures — such as Mexico's, where the Day of the Dead is an annual celebration — also have a more open and relaxed attitude to death.

However, in most modern Western cultures, we hide death away in hospitals, funeral homes, and crematoriums. It is excluded from polite conversations, TV programs, and newspapers. As a result, it may be that you have never contemplated your mortality. You may even unconsciously assume you are immortal, taking life for granted.

Anxiety. *Do you do occasionally or regularly contemplate death and find that it stirs feelings of anxiety and dread? Do you feel fearful at the prospect of leaving this world behind, including all the people and places you love and all the knowledge, achievements, and possessions you have accumulated? Perhaps you assume (as I* *once did) that death is the end, and feel anxiety at the prospect of abruptly shifting from this world of experience into oblivion. Even when you don't consciously contemplate death, you might have an undercurrent of death anxiety inside your mind, creating insecurity and vulnerability.*

In the light of your death anxiety, you might feel that life is absurd and meaningless. How can anything have any value in the face of death, when it can all be taken away — and will *be taken away — so easily?*

Acceptance. *Do you contemplate death with acceptance rather than anxiety? Do you acknowledge it as a natural process and feel happy to flow with it, comfortable with the idea that your body is a temporary physical form that will eventually dissolve? Do you calmly recognize that one day you'll have to give up everything you know and own and say goodbye to your loved ones? Perhaps you even sense that, rather than a terrible tragic event, your death may be a positive experience of detachment and liberation.*

AWAKENED ACCEPTANCE OF DEATH

In my research, I have found that acceptance of death is a defining characteristic of wakefulness. For example, I interviewed a man called Eric who had an awakening after a period of intense yoga practice. He told me that he had "no fear of death anymore. I'm not in a rush to die, but I'm not attached to the body and the life and the possessions. Life is a miracle and a mystery, and I'm happy with that." Similarly, an awakened man named Chris told me that he felt "very calm about [death]. . . . I would quite be willing to accept it if I was told my death was to come, even though I do not want to die just yet."

Awakened people don't fear death for two main reasons: because they don't perceive themselves as separate egos, and because they carry few (if any) psychological attachments. If you see yourself as the epicenter of the universe and are loaded with psychological attachments, then death is a terrible and tragic prospect. It represents the end of *everything*, the end of the world itself. It means the destruction of the empire you have built up throughout your life, like the fall of the Roman Empire after centuries of expansion.

However, awakened people travel lightly and transition easily. They perceive their existence as part of a vast network of being that will continue to flourish without them. They feel that they share their identity with the whole of the network, that something inside them is part of everything else. They sense that it is only their superficial identity that will dissolve away at death. There is a deeper, essential aspect of their being that will survive.

TRANSFORMATION THROUGH DEATH AWARENESS

Death awareness is so powerful that it's sometimes enough in itself to generate awakening. I have investigated many cases of transformation through turmoil triggered by direct encounters with death, such as a diagnosis of cancer or a heart attack. In fact, we've already discussed a few cases — for example, Tony, the launderette manager (in chapter 3) who had a transformation after a serious heart attack, and Irene (in chapter 5), who underwent an awakening after a cancer diagnosis. In Irene's case, transformation occurred straight after she received her diagnosis. As she told me, "It was the first time I'd seen death as a reality, and realized that life is just temporary.... The air was so clean and fresh and everything I looked at seemed so vibrant and vivid. The trees were so green and everything was so alive. I became aware of this energy radiating from the trees. I had a tremendous feeling of connectedness."

The poet and spiritual author Mark Nepo had a similar life-changing experience when he was diagnosed with cancer. He told me that, even now, more than thirty years later, "I'm simply glad to wake up and be here. I literally became a different person.... It was like going through a gate. You look back and then the gate you have come through has disappeared, and you know there is no going back. And having left that gate, the world is a completely different place."

When people are resuscitated after a short period of clinical death — for example, due to cardiac arrest — it's not uncommon for them to have a remarkable near-death experience. They often leave their bodies, witnessing medical procedures, then travel through darkness toward a light, with feelings of profound peace and love. They might encounter deceased relatives or spirit entities who impart wisdom and guidance. Sometimes they undergo a life review, in which all the events of their lives are replayed.

Near-death experiences almost always have a powerful awakening effect. People become less materialistic and more compassionate, more concerned with helping and serving others than with fulfilling their own desires and ambitions. They report a much greater capacity for joy and a heightened appreciation of beauty. They lose their fear of death, become more interested in spirituality, and sometimes even develop paranormal abilities. No doubt such transformations are partly due to the content of the experiences, which reveals that reality is much more meaningful and harmonious than they might have previously believed. But the transformation is probably also due to a powerful and direct encounter with death, similar to the experiences of cancer patients like Irene and Mark.

In many ways, an intense encounter with death is like a journey to the moon. It reveals the reality of our predicament as living beings, which is difficult for us to view objectively amid the triviality of everyday life. It makes us aware of the fragility and preciousness of life and the beauty and wonder of the world.

So now we're going to develop a harmonious relationship with death. We going to embrace our mortality, make friends with it, and invite it into our lives. We will cultivate a permanent, ongoing awareness of death, so that we can experience its transformational power and live fully in its light.

• CONTEMPLATIVE EXERCISE •

Life Is a Process

We live under assumptions of stability and separateness. We perceive time in terms of stable isolated moments, poised between the past and the future. We look around and perceive distinct objects and events. We perceive ourselves as distinct, separate individuals. However, in reality there is nothing but flow. Time is a continuous flow of nowness. Our experience consists of flowing processes of sensory information, meeting and merging with one another. And life itself is a process too. Your life is like a wave that forms on the surface of the ocean, builds up, rises, and breaks, then dissipates and disappears back into the ocean.

Let's contemplate the process of your life.

The process begins inside your mother's womb, when cells from your parents meet and merge. It's not clear where you were before then. Perhaps nowhere at all. Or perhaps your consciousness expressed itself in a different form, in another body.

Around nine months later, you enter the world and are separated from your mother's body to become an individual being. This is followed by a long period of growth and development, from childhood to adolescence, as you move toward your mature physical form.

During adulthood, as you flow with the process of life, your body changes. Your hair changes color and texture, your skin becomes rougher and looser. Slowly, some of your senses weaken. Your eyes lose their sharpness of vision; your hearing becomes less acute. Over time, some of the biological processes inside your body may grow unreliable. They may need some medical treatment to keep working properly.

However, there is no reason to feel loss or sadness as your body changes. Don't try to stall the process — accept it, flow with it. Celebrate it. Consider how fortunate you are to take this journey through time and space.

As the process continues, your body grows still more unreliable. Even if you've lived a healthy lifestyle, sooner or later, your body will deteriorate and stop functioning entirely. Your physical form will wither and dissolve away.

But again, there is no reason to feel a sense of loss. You have enjoyed the privilege of existence, of experiencing the glorious isness of the world. You emerged from the unmanifest, took form, and expressed your traits and potentials. It is equally glorious that your form will dissipate and become part of an ocean of pure consciousness again.

So as you live, view your life as a short, temporary, and fragile process. View your body as a temporary form that is undergoing constant change and will one day dissolve away.

View other people in this way too. Just as we often forget to see ourselves as mortal beings, we forget that our relatives and friends are also living temporary and fragile lives. Everyone you meet is in the midst of their own life process. Some have just begun the process; some are midway through; while others are nearing the end. They are all precious beings whom we are privileged to encounter, because they are only here for a short time, while their life process expresses itself.

My Temporary Life

I love my temporary life
because all its moments are precious
and all the people I share it with
are temporary precious beings
and the world in which I live my life
is full of temporary precious beauty
which will one day disappear, as I will disappear.

I love my temporary body
because it's full of fragile processes
millions of tiny miracles, occurring every second
all finely tuned and intertwined
to sustain my temporary life
allowing me to savor
the wonder of being in the world.

I love my temporary friends
because we're on the same journey, walking astride
helping and holding each other
relishing each other's company
because we know we can only walk together for a while.

I love my temporary life
because it's a dynamic process, in constant motion
ever since cells fused inside my mother's womb
flowing and unfolding, expanding and exploring
like a wave slowly forming then rising
that will one day slow down and dissipate
and merge with the ocean again.

DEATH REMINDERS

Many spiritual traditions emphasize the reality of death and encourage devotees to contemplate it. One of the core teachings of Buddhism is impermanence. All states and situations are continually changing and slowly dissolving, which is one of the reasons why life inevitably involves suffering. Whatever brings us happiness or security is bound to fade away at some point. There is nothing stable to grasp hold of.

The Buddha encouraged his monks to meditate in cemeteries or charnel grounds to remind themselves of the impermanence of life, that death is real and inevitable. In one of his sermons, the Satipatthana Sutta, the Buddha advised his monks that whenever they came across a dead body, they should tell themselves, "Verily, also my own body is of the same nature; such it will become and will not escape it." Through contemplating death in this way, a monk "lives detached, and clings to nothing in the world."

In a similar way, the sixth-century Christian teacher Saint Benedict counseled monks to "keep death daily before one's eyes." Monks would keep memento mori (death reminders), such as skulls, close at hand. The seventeenth-century pope Alexander VII kept a coffin in his bedroom and a skull on his desk to remind himself of his mortality. The Christian holy day of Ash Wednesday is a reminder of human mortality. Ashes are placed upon the foreheads of worshippers, while the priest recites a phrase from the Book of Genesis: "Remember, Man, that you are dust and unto dust, you shall return."

• LIFE PRACTICE •

Reminding Yourself of Death

I recommend that you follow similar practices to those I've just described. Take some time every day to contemplate death. It may not be socially acceptable in our death-denying culture, but feel free to keep a skull (if only a replica one) on your desk.

The early-twentieth-century spiritual teacher George Gurdjieff believed that every human being would wake up if they were told the exact date of their death. Of course, this is impossible to determine, but based on our age — and a few other factors, such as the longevity of our family members and our general health and lifestyle — we should be able to make a rough estimate. For example, I was born in 1967, and I live a fairly healthy lifestyle. The average age of my grandparents when they died was eighty-five. My father passed away at seventy-nine, my mother at seventy-seven. So I would roughly estimate my year of death as 2049, at eighty-two.

I suggest you do the same: estimate the year of your death, then write it down or print it on a large piece of paper. Pin the paper to the wall, perhaps in your office or bedroom. Contemplate the date every day, reminding yourself that life is temporary. Also remind yourself that this is your optimum date, which you will reach only if you're lucky enough to avoid any accidents or sudden injuries or illnesses. The real date of your death could be tomorrow, or next month, or next year. Death is always a potential occurrence, as much as it is an inevitable one.

It's also important to acknowledge and accept the deaths of others. Contemplate your relatives and friends who have passed away, acknowledging the inevitability of their passing. It was natural for their temporary forms to dissolve, and you were privileged to share part of their journey through life. Even if they died before reaching a full life span, that was natural too, since life is so fragile, dependent on so many different factors.

In addition, it's important to share the company of loved ones who are in the process of dying. Comfort and support them as their physical forms dissolve and consciousness passes from their bodies. Help them to face the reality of death, encouraging them into a mode of acceptance, so that they will pass serenely. At the same time, take the opportunity to face the reality of death yourself, contemplating that you will be in the same situation at some point.

If fortunate, you may be present at the precise moment that your relative or friend passes. In October 2021, I was present at the passing of my wife's mother, sitting at her bedside with my wife and children when she took her final breath. It was a profound experience, one that reminded me of witnessing the birth of my children. In both cases, I felt I was witnessing a miracle, a transition from one world to another. It struck me that birth and death are different forms of transformation, rather than opposites.

You may not be able to follow the Buddhist practice of meditating next to dead bodies (unless you work in a funeral home), but there is no reason why you shouldn't meditate — or at least contemplate death — at your local cemetery. Every couple of weeks or so, spend some time alone among the gravestones, reading the inscriptions, contemplating the fragility and impermanence of life. Sit down on a bench and meditate for a few minutes, clearing your mind of everyday concerns and associative thoughts. Then contemplate your finite physical form. Remind yourself that it's just a matter of time till you will die too. Then there will be nothing left of your physical form but a skeleton under the ground (if you choose to be buried) or a pile of ashes (if you choose to be cremated).

As you leave the cemetery, you will feel a new clarity and perspective, a stronger sense of meaning and purpose.

I recently wrote the following poem after visiting a local cemetery.

In the Cemetery

I walked through a cemetery this morning
in the clear winter sunshine, the grass crisp and white.
I paused by old, weathered gravestones
straining to read the faded names and dates
then found a corner of smooth, pristine stones
with inscriptions painfully fresh.

The cemetery was silent and still
but as I walked I heard voices
from different decades and centuries
whispering through the icy air.
Softly but urgently, the dead seemed to say:

If only we had realized that life is fragile
we would have savored each passing moment.
If only we had realized that life is brief
we would have seized every opportunity.
If only we had realized that life is precious
we would have stopped complaining and worrying
and lived with joy and love.

If only we had known the meaning of life
while we were still alive
then we would have truly lived.

There was no regret or disappointment.
The voices were tender, like loving grandparents
sharing the wisdom of their experience.

So don't be forgetful, as we were, I heard them whisper.
Wake in celebration every morning
go to sleep in gratitude every night
and appreciate each moment in between.
Don't live at the surface of your mind
amid resentment and regret and fear —
live from the deep space of your soul
sharing your light and love.
We realized too late; we spent our lives asleep.
But there's still time for you to wake up.

As I walked away from the gravestones, I looked up.
The sunlight streamed and charged through my body.
The endless blue sky filled me with space and stillness.
With each breath of cold air, I felt refreshed
gloriously awake and alive.

• CONTEMPLATIVE EXERCISE •

A Year to Live

I adapted the following exercise from the book *A Year to Live* by the poet, author, and Buddhist teacher Stephen Levine. In the book, Levine advises us to live the next year of life as if it's our final year, with guidelines to follow for each month. During the first part of the year, we should contemplate our attitude to death, then review our life, offering gratitude and forgiveness to those who we have shared it with. Later, we contemplate what will happen to our body after death, then write a will and an epitaph, along with letters and poems for the loved ones we are leaving. Toward the end of the year, we let go of our possessions and spend more time with relatives and friends, contemplating their mortality too. In the twelfth month, we say goodbye to our loved ones, thank our body for its perseverance, and prepare for death.

I created an abbreviated form of this exercise. This is ideally done as a group exercise, so if possible, ask a couple of friends or relatives to participate.

First, check today's date and write down the date of one year from now on a large piece of paper. This is the date of your death. You are going to die a year from today. You have only one year left in this body and in this world, 365 days left on the surface of this planet. Ponder this for a moment. You have just one year left to live as you wanted to live, to do the things you wanted to do, to say the things you wanted to say, to experience life in this form and in this world.

Contemplate how you're going to spend the final year of your life. Think in terms of different aspects of your life, such as relationships, lifestyle, and attitude. Ponder these areas and write down some of the changes you will make.

For example, how will your relationships change? Is there anyone you would like to make contact with, someone to apologize or make amends to? Would you like to repair a relationship that has broken down?

What changes will you make to your life on a day-to-day basis? Will you spend more time in nature or with your family? Will you devote your remaining time to writing or painting or some other creative activity? Will you give up some habits and adopt some new hobbies? Will you spend the time traveling?

Finally, how will your attitude to life change? What will you value more or feel grateful for? What attachments will you let go of? Will you become more present centered as you let go of the future and the past? Will you spend more time in a state of awareness, rather than in abstraction or absorption?

Write down all the changes you're going to make. If you're doing the exercise as a group, spend a few minutes sharing your intentions with one another. (It could be that you don't want to make any changes, which is fantastic, since it suggests that you are already living in an ideal, authentic way!)

The good news is that it's highly improbable you will die exactly a year from now. Of course, we can never be sure. It could be that you die later today, or tomorrow, or next month — or even precisely a year from today. But there is a good chance that, all being well, you have years and hopefully decades of life ahead of you.

Nevertheless, you should live the next year as if it actually is the final year of your life. Carry through with all the changes you've listed, all the intentions you've made.

A few changes may be impractical. For example, it may not be sensible to give up your job or leave university midway through your degree to travel the world. But you can certainly contact people from the past to repair relationships and spend more time in nature or with your children. You can take up new hobbies, devote yourself to creativity, and let go of your attachment to possessions or ambitions. You can appreciate every day of your life and feel love and gratitude toward everyone you spend your days with.

Follow through with all of these intentions. We never know when death will come, but it's always close at hand. We should always be prepared for it and always live in acknowledgment of it. Anything less is to live inauthentically.

• CONTEMPLATIVE EXERCISE •
The Fragility of Life

The Year to Live exercise is based on the temporary nature of life. Now I'd like to guide you through a short contemplation on the fragile nature of life, leading to a meditation in which we sense the eternal nature of the essence of our being.

Every moment, our survival depends on a vast array of intricate biological processes, all interacting to keep us healthy and conscious. These processes can become disrupted or imbalanced in two ways. First, they may be disrupted by external forces, when our bodies are damaged by other people or in accidents. Second, they can be disrupted by internal mechanical faults. Some of these faults may be congenital or genetic; others may be caused by an unhealthy lifestyle or deterioration due to age. If the disruption or imbalance is mild, it may be corrected — or at least contained — by medical treatment. However, if the disruption is serious, then the body may stop functioning, and we will die.

Let's meditate on the fragility of life in relation to these biological processes.

Consider some of the biological processes taking place inside you to keep you healthy and alive. Bring your awareness to some of these processes: your heart beating, your lungs breathing, your blood circulating, your kidneys cleansing your blood, your stomach and intestines digesting food. Consider more microcosmic processes, such as your immune system protecting you from germs and your billions of cells absorbing nutrients and metabolizing energy.

All these processes were set in motion when you were conceived or shortly afterward, while you were still inside your mother's womb. Ever since, they have worked incessantly to maintain your existence.

All the processes have been fine-tuned through millions of years of evolution, passed on to us from other living beings. For most of us, they are sturdy and reliable, provided we don't neglect or abuse our bodies. But eventually, the processes will begin to fail. In fact, they could randomly fail at any moment if we fall prey to an illness, injury, or accident. And no matter how well you eat or how much you exercise, no matter how much medical treatment you receive, at some point one or more of these processes will break down irreparably.

Ponder the fragility of your body and your life. Contemplate how fortunate you are to be alive in this world at this moment. The fact that you're alive right now is a miracle, given the complexity of all the myriad processes that sustain your life.

We don't know how long these processes will sustain your life. It's as if you're on a beautiful vacation but don't know how long it will last. All you know is that it will end at some point.

Now consider: What will happen when these processes do break down and your body can no longer function? Does your consciousness entirely depend on these biological processes? Will it be snuffed out like a candle when the processes stop?

Return to your inner space. Dive beneath the surface of your mind again, into the harmony of pure consciousness. Savor the stillness and spaciousness of your deep being, like the stillness of the deep ocean. Rest there, in peace, for a minute or two.

As you rest there, perhaps you can sense that the pure consciousness of your deep being is not contained by your body or your brain. It is not limited to them. It is not produced by them. It transcends them.

When the processes inside your body fail and can no longer support your physical existence, this pure consciousness will not disappear. It cannot disappear, because its not dependent on the processes.

This pure consciousness will endure beyond the death of your body. When your body dissolves, your personal consciousness will merge with universal consciousness, like a wave dissipating and reuniting with the ocean.

BEYOND DEATH

I've mentioned several times throughout this book that the different qualities of wakefulness intersect with and reinforce one another, and this is certainly true of death awareness. Becoming aware of the reality of death helps to release us from our psychological attachments. In the light of death, psychological attachments like ambitions, possessions, appearance, and career roles become meaningless. Death awareness also enhances presence. In the light of death, the future dissolves away, and the precious world around us becomes more real and beautiful, so that we spend much more time in awareness. Death awareness enhances gratitude too. The realization that everything in our lives — including our relatives and friends — is temporary and fragile helps us to transcend the taking for granted syndrome.

And after death? What happens then?

In a sense, it doesn't matter. While we're on our present journey, why should we concern ourselves with the next one? That would be like thinking ahead to your next vacation before your present one is over. The Buddha refused to answer abstract philosophical questions, stating that nothing mattered apart from transcending suffering and finding inner peace. Perhaps he also felt that philosophical questions were a distraction from the nowness of experience.

But it's worth noting that most spiritually awakened people do sense that there is some kind of life after death, even if they don't have a clear idea about what form it will take. This is another reason why they transcend fear of death: because they sense that death doesn't mean the end, that it's not a termination but a transformation. They may even intuit that dying is not an event to be feared, but rather a process of liberation, bringing deep serenity. As a woman called Helen told me, "I'm not afraid of death at all — in fact in some ways I think it's something to look forward to, a kind of liberation." A woman named Marita described dying as moving "outside of time, outside of space… like stepping outside of prison walls."

So as awareness and acceptance of death enhance your wakefulness, your perspective on death may well change, in the same way that looking at a painting for a long time makes you see it in a different way. As your wakefulness increases, you will see more and more clearly that death is not a point of extinction or a fall into nothingness. It is not the end of our journey, but the beginning of a new adventure.

10

THE ENDLESS ADVENTURE

Throughout this book, I've offered meditations to cultivate the qualities of wakefulness — to develop disidentification, gratitude, presence, altruism, and so on. However, before I step down from my role as spiritual guide, I would like to highlight the importance of meditation as a general life practice.

Any form of meditation, when practiced regularly, helps to cultivate all the qualities of wakefulness we've explored. Meditation encourages disidentification and presence by turning our attention away from the thought mind. It encourages altruism by decentering us from our own mental space and connecting us with other people and the natural world. Meditation encourages acceptance by freeing us from mental stories about what's "wrong" with our life situation or how our lives "should" be. It also helps to free us from psychological attachments by opening access to the essential well-being that lies beneath our attachments.

So while I don't want to overburden you with spiritual practices, I recommend any traditional meditation practice as a way of reinforcing and integrating the different qualities of wakefulness. Just sitting quietly for fifteen to twenty minutes each morning, focusing on a mantra or on your breathing or using an open meditation technique of observing your thoughts and feelings, is a great way of supporting your overall spiritual development.

It's also worth remembering that, as I pointed out at the end of chapter 7, there are many types of active meditation, such as running, swimming, and walking in the countryside. Such activities can also help to consolidate and integrate our wakefulness.

EMERGENT QUALITIES OF WAKEFULNESS

The fact that meditation has such wide-ranging effects is another illustration of how interrelated all the qualities of wakefulness are. As I've demonstrated several times, they all inform and influence one another. As we cultivate each quality individually, the other qualities develop in parallel. Some qualities are more intertwined than others — for example, presence is strongly linked to disidentification, and embracing mortality is powerfully linked to detachment. You can think of the eight qualities as members of a family, some of whom have closer relationships than others, but all of whom are related. And if any member of the family develops in a positive way, it has a positive effect on the family as a whole.

Another aspect of this interdependence is that as we develop the eight qualities, new qualities emerge through their interaction. This doesn't mean that these emergent qualities are in any way less important than the first eight qualities. In fact, they include some of the most fundamental and overt traits of wakefulness. To continue the family metaphor, it's as if offspring are born, expanding the family, and some of the additions become the most prominent members of the family.

I've already discussed a few of these emergent qualities in connection with the characteristics that give rise to them. For example, I mentioned that as we disidentify with the thought mind, we develop inner quietness. Without the fuel of attention, thoughts slow down, and space opens up inside us. I also noted that as we develop presence, we gain the ability to *be* and no longer fear inactivity and solitude. On the contrary, we find doing nothing to be intensely pleasurable. These qualities — inner quietness and the ability to be — are two of the most significant traits of awakened individuals.

Another important emergent quality of wakefulness — one that, again, we've already touched on — is the transcendence of separateness. We become aware that we're not isolated mental entities, trapped inside our mental space. We share our spiritual essence with the whole universe, with every material object and every living being. We sense that we are waves on the surface of the ocean, part of the oneness of the universe.

Almost every quality of awakening helps us to transcend separateness. Disidentification and presence lift us out of our mental space, connecting us to the world; gratitude and altruism make us less self-oriented and more connected to other beings; acceptance makes us one with the reality of our lives; detachment weakens the structure of the ego; and so on.

As we awaken, we also gain a sense of the interconnectedness of everything we perceive. We sense a subtle resonance that links both natural and human-made objects. They share the same nature and are a part of something greater and more fundamental. At a high intensity of wakefulness, the nature of this interconnection becomes clear: all things are manifestations of an underlying spirit or consciousness. They stem from the same spiritual source and share the same spiritual essence. Like us, they are all waves on the surface of an ocean of spirit. Like us, they all flow out of the ocean and are one with each other, just as they are one with the ocean itself.

Another emergent quality is heightened awareness, or intensified perception. Through becoming more present, disidentifying from the thought mind, and transcending the taking for granted syndrome, we perceive the beautiful isness of the world. The world begins to shine with radiance. Trees and plants and even inanimate objects glow with vitality. Gray skies and drizzling rain seem dramatic and beautiful. After awakening, it's impossible for us to feel bored, since there are always beautiful objects and fascinating phenomena to perceive.

Other emergent qualities manifest themselves more subtly, through our lifestyle and behavior. One change — which I've touched on but not addressed directly — is a shift to a simple, nonmaterialistic lifestyle. An impulse for simplicity replaces the desire for possessions. An impulse to contribute replaces the desire to accumulate wealth or power or success. The need to accumulate is gone, because we no longer have a fragile, separate identity to support or a sense of lack to try to fill.

OTHER CHANGES THAT COME WITH AWAKENING

As you awaken, your relationships will also change, becoming more authentic and intimate. You won't feel the need to wear a mask or play a role, to pretend to be someone you're not. Your friendships will be based on honesty and trust, on sharing your deepest thoughts and feelings. You will find it easier to express affection and love.

In all your dealings with other people, you will become less judgmental and more tolerant and compassionate. You'll be much less likely to fall out with neighbors, to have arguments with colleagues, or to get irritated with other drivers or passengers. Harmony will pervade all your relationships, from the intimate to the casual.

A sense of authenticity will pervade your whole life. Your behavior will stem from your deepest impulses and your moral principles, rather than from the need to please others or follow conventions. Your lifestyle will be aligned with your own true nature, rather than with societal expectations. Other people may consider you eccentric because of your spontaneity and individuality, but you won't mind.

You'll also develop a wide-ranging view of reality. As disidentification and presence decenter you from your ego, and as gratitude and altruism connect you to others, your awareness of the world will expand. You will no longer see the world through a lens of egocentrism, preoccupied with your personal problems to the exclusion of everything else. You'll stop viewing yourself as the center of the universe. Social and global issues will be as important as, if not more important than, your personal issues. You will be aware of how your life choices affect others and the Earth itself. (Throughout this book, I've tried to help you cultivate this overview awareness by offering contemplative exercises, such as viewing the Earth from space, expanding your circle of concern, and transcending group identity.)

However, perhaps the most obvious emergent quality of awakening is an overall sense of well-being. In the normal sleep state, human life is full of suffering, as the Buddha noted. Most people live in a state of continual inner discord, which they try to distract themselves from with activities and entertainments. But as we awaken, harmony fills our beings and our lives. The sources of discord — the restless negativity and separateness of the thought mind, the heaviness of psychological attachments — fade away, replaced by a natural ease. The undercurrent of anxiety dissipates from our minds, replaced by spacious stillness and radiant well-being.

THE CHALLENGES OF AWAKENING

When awakening occurs suddenly and dramatically, it can sometimes be challenging. Particularly if people don't have a background in spirituality, they may be slightly confused and wonder if they've gone crazy. Sudden awakenings can also bring about psychological disturbances. As our old identity dissolves, some psychological processes may be affected, so that we find it difficult to concentrate, to remember things, or to relate to other people. It may take time for our new identity to establish itself and for these processes to function properly again. If we don't understand the awakening process, we (and others around us) may confuse these disturbances with a breakdown. In the worst-case scenario, we may end up being diagnosed with a psychiatric condition and even committed to a psychiatric hospital.

However, when awakening occurs gradually, through the kinds of structured processes I've described in this book, it usually proceeds fairly smoothly. I sometimes use the analogy of fame: When it occurs suddenly, fame is often difficult to adjust to, because of the pressure of constant attention and lack of privacy. But when a person becomes famous over many years, they adapt to it as they go along, so that it isn't destabilizing. In a similar way, progressive awakening allows for understanding and adjustment. It enables us to integrate the changes that arise. New psychological structures establish themselves slowly, without disruption, like new employees who receive training and supervision before officially taking on their roles.

Nevertheless, don't be surprised if some challenges do arise in the process of awakening. The new landscape of wakefulness may feel a little disorienting. As your awareness opens to the world, you may sometimes feel *too* sensitive, slightly overwhelmed by the perceptions, impressions, and experiences that flood through your senses. As you become more empathic and compassionate, you may sometimes feel overwhelmed with awareness of the sufferings or even joys of others. Your overview awareness may bring some despondency about the state of the world or the future of humanity. Within your own being, as your ego boundaries soften, you may find that repressed inner pain or trauma rises to the surface.

If such challenges do arise, view them as part of a natural process of adjustment. Like a person who moves from the plains to a mountain landscape, you may well experience some altitude sickness before adjusting to the rarefied new climate. You might initially feel disoriented by the open space and panoramic views. But as your wakefulness stabilizes and intensifies, you will integrate the changes. So relax and allow the process of adjustment to unfold. You will soon settle down, to enjoy your freedom and relish the beauty of the landscape.

THE CONTINUUM OF WAKEFULNESS

Once your new awakened self has become established, you'll gain a sense of inner stability and deep well-being. You will still feel the pain of others and respond with altruistic action. You'll still feel deeply concerned about social and global issues and contribute to the effort to alleviate them. But you won't feel overwhelmed. Your concern won't translate into inner pain or disturbance. Awareness of suffering won't hurt you, in the same way that the strongest wind and heaviest rain can't damage a sturdy, deep-rooted tree.

However, don't expect your wakefulness to completely immunize you against what Shakespeare called "the slings and arrows of outrageous fortune." Don't expect to be unmoved when loved ones pass away, relationships end, or projects fail. You'll still feel sadness, disappointment, and even anger in some situations. But provided you don't identify with them, such reactions will naturally arise and pass away. Emotional reactions will take on the same status as physical pain. They will simply express themselves and then fade.

In a similar way, don't expect awakening to immediately make you a perfect person, completely free of faults. You may carry over some old negative personality traits, such as a lack of confidence in certain situations or a tendency toward competitiveness or jealousy. Such traits may continue as habits and take some time to fade away. But so long as we are conscious of them and don't identify with them, they will grow weaker.

Remember that wakefulness is a continuum. There are different degrees of wakefulness, just as there are different levels of a mountain. As your wakefulness intensifies, negative personality traits will become weaker, and you'll become less disturbed by negative events and emotions. At the same time, your experience of both the core and emergent qualities of wakefulness will intensify. Your gratitude and altruism will intensify. You will experience greater presence, acceptance, and detachment. A sense of connection to the world will expand into a sense of oneness. Awareness of the beauty and suchness of the world will transform into awareness of a spiritual energy that shines through all things and brings them into oneness. A sense of empathy for others will grow into unconditional love.

A JOURNEY WITHOUT END

I don't believe we ever reach a point of complete wakefulness. We keep exploring through wider and deeper expanses of awareness.

We keep climbing through ever more rarefied altitudes without ever reaching a specific peak.

So don't expect to arrive at a destination or a final place of rest. As your wakefulness intensifies, you will continue to discover new aspects of reality, to uncover fresh aspects of your own being, and to develop new depths of intimacy and authenticity with others. The process ends only when our life ends — and perhaps not even then.

And of course, the adventure of awakening was never specifically *ours* in any case. The impulse to awaken is not an egoic personal desire to become more productive or perfect or happy; it is a deep-rooted evolutionary urge to expand awareness, to grow toward a more harmonious state. It is an extension of a journey that began billions of years ago, when the universe first formed, then progressed through the first atomic structures, the first lifeforms, and then through the ever-increasing complexity and sentience of living beings as they evolved.

We undertake the adventure of awakening collectively. Some people are still preparing for their individual journeys. Some are further along than others. Some have made significant progress already. But every human being is part of the adventure, whether they're aware of it or not. We awaken with each other and for each other — for our whole species, for other species, and on behalf of the universe itself.

As more and more of us undergo awakening, the journey will flow more smoothly. The collective momentum of awakening will increase. The landscape of wakefulness will become more accessible and familiar to all human beings, until eventually it becomes our species' home.

In the process, our inner transformation will transform the world. From the new harmony within us, a new harmonious world will naturally form, just as our old inner discord created a world full of conflict and chaos. For us both individually and as a species, life will no longer be a frenzied struggle, full of stress and fear, but a glorious adventure, full of grace and joy.

It has been a privilege to be your guide. Blessings to you, as we both continue our journeys, together in the oneness of spirit.

ACKNOWLEDGMENTS

A number of the exercises and meditations in this book are adapted from my audio program *Return to Harmony*. Thanks to Sounds True for permission to adapt the material.

Thanks to all the participants of my workshops and courses since 2017, where I developed the content of this book. Your responses to the exercises encouraged me to create the book.

I am deeply grateful to the team at New World Library, who have again been so supportive and cooperative and pleasant to work with — the true embodiment of a spiritually oriented publisher!

I'm also deeply grateful to Eckhart Tolle, for his longstanding support of my teachings and for his support of this book in particular.

EXERCISES AND MEDITATIONS

CHAPTER 1: GUIDELINES

CHAPTER 2: DISIDENTIFICATION

CHAPTER 3: GRATITUDE

CHAPTER 4: PRESENCE

CHAPTER 5: ALTRUISM

CHAPTER 6: ACCEPTANCE

CHAPTER 7: INTEGRATION

CHAPTER 8: DETACHMENT

CHAPTER 9: EMBRACING MORTALITY

NOTES

CHAPTER 2: DISIDENTIFICATION

p. 20 *"My mind had slowed down"*: Steve Taylor, *The Leap: The Psychology of Spiritual Awakening* (Novato, CA: New World Library, 2017), 110.

p. 20 *"because I notice the thoughts"*: Taylor, *The Leap*, 190.

CHAPTER 3: GRATITUDE

p. 39 *"Happiness is being aware"*: Taylor, *The Leap*, 165.

p. 40 *"I feel like I'm living"*: Taylor, *The Leap*, 166.

p. 40 *"I love talking to young people"*: Taylor, *The Leap*, 167.

p. 40 *"What you should do"*: Taylor, *The Leap*, 165–66.

p. 43 *"I just feel light"*: Steve Taylor, *Extraordinary Awakenings: When Trauma Leads to Transformation* (Novato, CA: New World Library, 2021), 169.

p. 43 *"real gratitude for the birds"*: Taylor, *The Leap*, 203.

p. 46 *"dynamic, overwhelming"*: Eugene A. Cernan, interview by Rebecca Wright, December 11, 2007, NASA Johnson Space Center Oral History Project, https://history collection.jsc.nasa.gov/JSCHistoryPortal/history /oral_histories/CernanEA/CernanEA_12-11-07.htm.

p. 47 *"interconnected euphoria"*: "Space: The Greening of the Astronauts," *Time*, December 11, 1972, https://content.time .com/time/subscriber/article/0,33009,878100-3,00.html.

p. 47 *"You realize that"*: Rusty Schweikhart, "No Frame, No Boundaries: Connecting with the Whole Planet — from Space," *In Context*, Summer 1983, https://www.context.org/iclib/ic03/schweick/.

p. 47 *"Since that time I have not"*: David Sington, dir., *In the Shadow of the Moon* (London: Dox Productions, 2006).

CHAPTER 4: PRESENCE

p. 61 *"It's so nice just to sit"*: Taylor, *The Leap*, 205.

p. 61 *"I don't get bored anymore"*: Taylor, *The Leap*, 206.

p. 61 *"I can be on my own"*: Taylor, *The Leap*, 206.

p. 82 *"Being slow — physically moving"*: Steve Taylor, *Out of the Darkness: From Turmoil to Transformation* (London: Hay House, 2011), 68.

CHAPTER 5: ALTRUISM

p. 87 *"a shift in focus"*: Taylor, *The Leap*, 207.

p. 87 *"The purpose of my life"*: Taylor, *Extraordinary Awakenings*, 29.

p. 87 *"I want to make sure"*: Taylor, *Extraordinary Awakenings*, 95.

p. 97 *"I realized that it wasn't serving any purpose"*: Steve Taylor, "Are You Ready to Forgive?," *Psychology Today* blog, July 18, 2014, https://www.psychologytoday.com/us/blog/out-the-darkness/201407/are-you-ready-forgive.

p. 100 *"Forgiveness is an absolute necessity"*: Archbishop Desmond Tutu, "Without Forgiveness There Is No Future," foreword to Robert D. Enright and Joanna North, eds., *Exploring Forgiveness* (Madison, WI: University of Wisconsin Press, 1998), xiii.

p. 102 *"a citizen of the cosmos"*: Taylor, *The Leap*, 94.
p. 102 *"Now I just watch"*: Taylor, *The Leap*, 201.
p. 103 *"You look down there"*: Schweikhart, "No Frame, No Boundaries."
p. 108 *"I experienced in that moment"*: Paul Marshall, *Mystical Encounters with the Natural World* (Oxford: Oxford University Press, 2005), 61–62.
p. 108 *"A most curious but overwhelming"*: Alister Hardy, *The Spiritual Nature of Man* (Oxford: Clarendon Press, 1979), 53.

CHAPTER 6: ACCEPTANCE

p. 115 *"We whites squirmed"*: Edward T. Hall, *The Dance of Life* (New York: Anchor Press, 1984), 132–33.
p. 116 *the best way of dealing*: Taylor, *Out of the Darkness*, 73.
p. 125 *people "are disturbed not by things"*: Epictetus, *The Enchiridion*, trans. Thomas W. Higginson (New York: Liberal Arts Press, 1948), chapter 5, https://www.gutenberg.org/files/45109/45109-h/45109-h.htm.
p. 126 *"Let go, man, let go"*: Taylor, *Out of the Darkness*, 73.

CHAPTER 7: INTEGRATION

p. 134 *"faeces, urine, menstruation, nails"*: Sidney Spenser, *Mysticism in World Religion* (London: Penguin, 1960), 338.
p. 134 *"O I say these are not"*: Walt Whitman, "I Sing the Body Electric," in *Leaves of Grass (*1855; reprint, New York: Signet Books, 1980*)*, 105.
p. 135 *"aware of all the different"*: Taylor, *Out of the Darkness*, 143.
p. 135 *"I became a vegetarian"*: Taylor, *Out of the Darkness*, 25.
p. 146 *"in awe of my body"*: Taylor, *Out of the Darkness*, 68.

CHAPTER 8: DETACHMENT

p. 151 *"the same in pleasure and pain"*: Juan Mascaró, ed. and trans., *The Bhagavad Gita* (1962; reprint, London: Penguin, 1988), 68.

p. 154 *the happiest age group*: Office for National Statistics, "Measuring National Well-being: At What Age Is Personal Well-being the Highest?," Census 2021, https://www.ons.gov.uk/peoplepopulationandcommunity/wellbeing/articles/measuringnationalwellbeing/atwhatageispersonalwellbeingthehighest.

p. 156 *she was living "Life Two"*: Taylor, *Out of the Darkness*, 67.

p. 157 *"like the transformation"*: Taylor, *Out of the Darkness*, 55.

p. 157 *"My whole psyche changed"*: Taylor, *Extraordinary Awakenings*, 169.

CHAPTER 9: EMBRACING MORTALITY

p. 178 *"no fear of death anymore"*: Taylor, *The Leap*, 196.

p. 178 *"very calm about [death]"*: Taylor, *The Leap*, 196.

p. 179 *"It was the first time"*: Taylor, *Out of the Darkness*, 144-145.

p. 180 *"I'm simply glad to wake up"*: Taylor, *Extraordinary Awakenings*, 100.

p. 184 *"Verily, also my own body"*: Vipassana Fellowship, "The Nine Cemetery Contemplations," https://www.vipassana.com/meditation/foundations_of_mindfulness_part2.html.

p. 184 *"keep death daily"*: St. Benedict, *The Rule of St. Benedict* (London: SPCK, 1931), 6.

p. 185 *"Remember, Man, that you"*: Gen. 3:19.

p. 188 *I adapted the following*: Stephen Levine, *A Year to Live* (New York: Harmony, 1998).

p. 194 *"I'm not afraid of death"*: Taylor, *The Leap*, 197.

p. 194 *"outside of time"*: Taylor, *The Leap*, 197.

BIBLIOGRAPHY

Cernan, Eugene A. Interview by Rebecca Wright, December 11, 2007. NASA Johnson Space Center Oral History Project. https://historycollection.jsc.nasa.gov/JSCHistoryPortal/history/oral_histories/CernanEA/CernanEA 12-11-07.htm.

Hall, Edward T. *The Dance of Life*. New York: Anchor Press, 1984.

Hardy, Alister. *The Spiritual Nature of Man*. Oxford: Clarendon Press, 1979.

Levine, Stephen. *A Year to Live*. New York: Harmony, 1998.

Marshall, Paul. *Mystical Encounters with the Natural World*. Oxford: Oxford University Press, 2005.

Mascaró, Juan, ed. and trans. *The Bhagavad Gita*. 1962. Reprint, London: Penguin, 1988.

Office for National Statistics. "Measuring National Well-Being: At What Age Is Personal Well-Being the Highest?" UK Office for National Statistics, Census 2021. https://www.ons.gov.uk/peoplepopulationandcommunity/wellbeing/articles/measuringnationalwellbeing/atwhatageispersonalwellbeingthehighest.

Schweickart, Rusty. "No Frame, No Boundaries: Connecting with the Whole Planet — from Space." *In Context*, Summer 1983. https://www.context.org/iclib/ic03/schweick/.

Sington, David, dir. *In the Shadow of the Moon*. London: Dox Productions, 2006.

"Space: The Greening of the Astronauts." *Time*, December 11, 1972. https://content.time.com/time/subscriber/article/0,33009,878100-3,00.html.

Spenser, Sidney. *Mysticism in World Religion*. London: Penguin, 1960.

St. Benedict, *The Rule of St. Benedict*. London: SPCK, 1931.

Taylor, Steve. *Extraordinary Awakenings: When Trauma Leads to Transformation*. Novato, CA: New World Library, 2021.

———. *The Leap: The Psychology of Spiritual Awakening*. Novato, CA: New World Library, 2017.

———. *Out of the Darkness: From Turmoil to Transformation*. London: Hay House, 2011.

Vipassana Fellowship. "The Nine Cemetery Contemplations." https://www.vipassana.com/meditation/foundations_of_mindfulness_part2.html.

Whitman, Walt. "I Sing the Body Electric." In *Leaves of Grass*. 1855. Reprint, New York: Signet Books, 1980.

ABOUT THE AUTHOR

Steve Taylor, PhD, is the author of several bestselling books on psychology and spirituality, including *Extraordinary Awakenings* and *The Leap*. He is also the author of three books of spiritual poetry, including *The Clear Light* and *The Calm Center*, and the audio program *Return to Harmony*. Taylor is a senior lecturer in psychology at Leeds Beckett University in the United Kingdom and writes the popular blog *Out of the Darkness* for *Psychology Today*. He lives in Manchester, England.

StevenMTaylor.com

THE ADVENTURE ONLINE COURSE

Steve Taylor leads an online course called *The Adventure*, based on the contents of this book. The course runs over eight weeks and includes meditations, exercises, poems, and discussions. Check his website at StevenMTaylor.com for details on how to enroll.

About Eckhart Tolle Editions

Eckhart Tolle Editions was launched in 2015 to publish life-changing works, both old and new, that have been personally selected by Eckhart Tolle. This imprint of New World Library presents books that can powerfully aid in transforming consciousness and awakening readers to a life of purpose and presence.

Learn more about Eckhart Tolle at

www.eckharttolle.com

NEW WORLD LIBRARY is dedicated to publishing books and other media that inspire and challenge us to improve the quality of our lives and the world.

We are a socially and environmentally aware company. We recognize that we have an ethical responsibility to our readers, our authors, our staff members, and our planet.

We serve our readers by creating the finest publications possible on personal growth, creativity, spirituality, wellness, and other areas of emerging importance. We serve our authors by working with them to produce and promote quality books that reach a wide audience. We serve New World Library employees with generous benefits, significant profit sharing, and constant encouragement to pursue their most expansive dreams.

Whenever possible, we print our books with soy-based ink on 100 percent postconsumer-waste recycled paper. We power our offices with solar energy and contribute to nonprofit organizations working to make the world a better place for us all.

Our products are available wherever books are sold.

customerservice@NewWorldLibrary.com
Phone: 415-884-2100 or 800-972-6657
Orders: Ext. 110 • Catalog requests: Ext. 110
Fax: 415-884-2199
NewWorldLibrary.com

Scan below to access our newsletter
and learn more about our books and authors.